simply bill
bill granger

photography by petrina tinslay

MURDOCH BOOKS

contents

I'm not a chef but I do cook every day. Some days I cook for pleasure and some days for fuel. In today's world we are bombarded with so much of everything when what we really need is very simple — our health and time to enjoy our friends, loved ones and ourselves. For me, food manages to pull all these things together. Food is my great pleasure: it anchors all the parts of my life. What I cook is dependent on many different factors: time, energy levels, what's in the shops... the meal I prepare on a Monday night is different to the celebration lunch I make for friends, but all my food is similarly pared back. For me, the greatest sophistication is in simplicity. I hope that in this collection of meals and menus you'll find something delicious for every day.

weekdays

Weekdays for me are all about planning — shopping at the weekend so that there are basics in the pantry, and just picking up a couple of fresh ingredients on the way home. Weekday suppers are eaten around the kitchen table with the family, occasionally off a tray on my lap in front of the telly or with friends who drop in for a last-minute dinner. They can be the great 'freezables' (stews, braises and soups) or a quick pasta or salad assemblage. Weekday evenings in our house are often mad, hurried times and like everyone I have a selection of straightforward, usually one-dish, meals that I can cook with my eyes closed (and sometimes do). Here are a few of them.

spaghetti with cherry tomatoes, ricotta, spinach and pecorino

750 g (1 lb 10 oz) cherry tomatoes
4 garlic cloves, sliced
1 red onion, thinly sliced
small handful fresh oregano
100 ml (3½ fl oz) extra virgin olive oil
500 g (1 lb 2 oz) fresh spaghetti
50 g (1¾ oz) baby English spinach
200 g (7 oz) fresh ricotta
freshly ground black pepper

to serve
75 g (2¾ oz) pecorino cheese, grated

Preheat the oven to 180°C (350°F/Gas 4). Put the tomatoes, garlic, onion and oregano on a baking tray and drizzle with the oil. Roast for 20–25 minutes or until wilted.

Cook the pasta in a large saucepan of boiling salted water until *al dente*. Drain and toss with the tomato mixture, spinach and half the ricotta. Divide among serving bowls and top with the remaining ricotta and some freshly ground pepper. Serve with the grated pecorino. Serves 4

This is a dish that's very adaptable to whatever happens to be in your fridge. Chicken instead of prawns is an easy variation.

rice noodles with prawns and lime

125 g (4½ oz) dry rice noodles
10 raw prawns (shrimp), peeled, deveined and halved lengthways
2 tablespoons korma curry paste
2 tablespoons light-flavoured oil (I like canola)
2 eggs, lightly beaten
4 spring onions (scallions), cut into lengths
125 ml (4 fl oz/½ cup) chicken stock
2 tablespoons soy sauce

to serve
coriander (cilantro) sprigs
lime wedges

Put the noodles in a bowl and soak in hot water for about 5 minutes or until soft. Drain well and set aside. Put the prawns in a bowl with the curry paste and stir until the prawns are well coated.

Heat a large frying pan or wok over high heat. Add 1 tablespoon of the oil and pour in the eggs. Leave to set for 10 seconds, then push the eggs to the centre of the pan, almost scrambling them. When the eggs are about three-quarters cooked, remove them from the pan.

Wipe out the pan or wok with paper towels and return to the heat. Add the remaining oil and the prawns and stir gently for 1–2 minutes, then add the spring onions and stir-fry for 1 minute. Add the stock, soy sauce and noodles and stir-fry for 1–2 minutes until heated through. Add the egg, toss to combine and remove from the heat. Divide between two bowls and serve with coriander sprigs and lime wedges. Serves 2

minute steaks with lemon

4 minute steaks (100 g/3½ oz each)
olive oil
sea salt
freshly ground black pepper

to serve
lemon wedges
green beans with tomatoes and chilli,
 below

Heat a frying pan over high heat. Brush the steaks with olive oil and sprinkle with salt and pepper. Cook for 1 minute each side, or until cooked to your liking. Serve with lemon wedges and green beans with tomatoes and chilli. Serves 4

green beans with tomatoes and chilli

2 tablespoons olive oil
3 garlic cloves, thinly sliced
1 small red chilli, chopped or
 ¼ teaspoon dried red chilli flakes
sea salt
500 g (1 lb 2 oz) tomatoes, chopped
500 g (1 lb 2 oz) green beans, trimmed
freshly ground black pepper

to serve
chopped fresh flat-leaf (Italian) parsley

Heat a pan over medium–high heat and add the olive oil, garlic, chilli and a good sprinkling of salt. Cook, stirring, for 30 seconds until the garlic is golden. Add the tomatoes, reduce the heat to medium and cook for 10 minutes, stirring occasionally.

Meanwhile, place a large saucepan of water over high heat and bring to the boil. Add the beans and cook for 4 minutes. Drain and add to the tomatoes with some freshly ground black pepper. Toss well and cook for a couple of minutes longer. Sprinkle with parsley. Serves 4

You can't scrimp on quality when you're making fish cakes. Always use good-quality whole-egg mayonnaise or make your own. I like to use blue-eye cod for the fish.

fish cakes

15 g (½ oz) butter
2 celery stalks, finely chopped
1 leek or onion, finely chopped
750 g (1 lb 10 oz) firm white fish fillets, skin removed, pin-boned and diced
250 g (9 oz/1 cup) whole-egg mayonnaise
3 tablespoons snipped chives
small handful chopped fresh flat-leaf (Italian) parsley
2–3 drops Tabasco sauce
360 g (12¾ oz/4½ cups) fresh wholemeal breadcrumbs

sea salt
freshly ground black pepper
125 g (4½ oz/1 cup) plain (all-purpose) flour
3 eggs, beaten
125 ml (4 fl oz/½ cup) light-flavoured oil (I like light olive or canola)

to serve
watercress and grapefruit salad, below

Melt the butter in a frying pan over medium–low heat, add the celery and cook for 1 minute to soften slightly. Add the leek and cook for 1–2 minutes. Set aside to cool a little and then tip into a bowl.

Add the fish to the bowl with the mayonnaise, chives, parsley, Tabasco and 250 g (9 oz/3 cups) of the breadcrumbs. Season with salt and freshly ground black pepper. Mix together well and form into 12 patties.

Put the flour, beaten egg and remaining breadcrumbs in separate bowls. Coat the fish cakes first in the flour, then in the beaten egg and finally in the breadcrumbs. Refrigerate for 30 minutes to firm a little.

Preheat the oven to 180°C (350°F/Gas 4). Heat the oil in a frying pan over medium–high heat. Fry the fish cakes in batches for 1–2 minutes on each side until crisp. Transfer to a baking tray and place in the oven for 5–6 minutes until cooked through. Serve warm with watercress and grapefruit salad. Serves 4

watercress and grapefruit salad

2 grapefruit
90 g (3¼ oz/3 cups) watercress, trimmed
2 radishes, sliced

2 teaspoons salted capers, rinsed
3 tablespoons extra virgin olive oil
sea salt
freshly ground black pepper

Segment the grapefruit, removing the pith, and put in a bowl with the watercress, radish and capers. Squeeze the juice from the remaining grapefruit pulp until you have 1½ tablespoons. Whisk with the olive oil, salt and pepper to make a dressing and toss with the salad. Serves 4

curried chicken rice

1 kg (2 lb 4 oz) chicken pieces on the
  bone, with skin
2 tablespoons Indian curry powder
1 tablespoon olive oil
1 onion, chopped
2 garlic cloves, crushed
300 g (10½ oz/1½ cups) basmati rice
750 ml (26 fl oz/3 cups) chicken stock

to serve
150 g (5½ oz) plain yoghurt
cucumber and lime salad, right

Preheat the oven to 200°C (400°F/Gas 6). Put the chicken in a large bowl, add the curry powder and toss to coat well. Place a heavy-based casserole with a tight-fitting lid over medium heat. Add the oil and chicken pieces and cook until they are sealed and browned all over. Remove the chicken to a plate.

Add the onion and garlic to the casserole and cook until the onion is soft and pale golden. Add the rice, stir to combine and cook for 2 minutes. Put the chicken back into the casserole in a single layer over the rice and carefully pour in the stock.

Put on the lid and bake in the oven for 45 minutes or until the rice is tender and has absorbed all the liquid and the chicken is cooked through. Serve with yoghurt and cucumber and lime salad. Serves 4

You can make a simple cucumber and lime salad that is great with this dish (and with most other Indian-flavoured meats). Toss together 2 chopped Lebanese cucumbers, 3 sliced spring onions (scallions) and a small handful of whole mint leaves. Dress with 1 tablespoon of olive oil, the juice of a lime and a dash of sea salt.

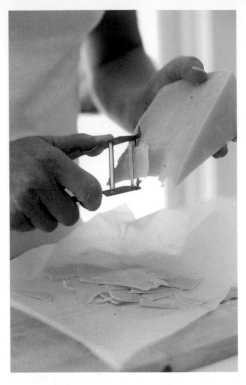

I really like to use pecorino sometimes, rather than the more obvious parmesan. Pecorino is an Italian sheep's milk cheese. You can either grate it or use a vegetable peeler to make shavings.

penne with eggplant and chilli

1 large eggplant (aubergine), sliced
80 ml (2½ fl oz/⅓ cup) olive oil
sea salt
4 garlic cloves, thinly sliced
2 red chillies, thinly sliced
2 x 400 g (14 oz) tins chopped tomatoes
freshly ground black pepper
500 g (1 lb 2 oz) penne
small handful chopped fresh flat-leaf
 (Italian) parsley

to serve
30 g (1 oz) pecorino cheese, grated or
 shaved

Preheat the grill (broiler). Arrange the eggplant on a baking tray, brush liberally with half of the oil and sprinkle with salt on both sides. Grill for 3–6 minutes on each side or until golden brown and cooked. When the eggplant is cool enough to handle, cut into small cubes.

Meanwhile, place a frying pan over medium heat. Add the rest of the oil and sauté the garlic, chilli and a little salt for 1 minute. Add the tomatoes and pepper and simmer for 10–15 minutes. Gently fold through the eggplant.

Meanwhile, cook the pasta in a large saucepan of boiling salted water until *al dente*. Drain well and toss with the sauce and parsley. Serve with the pecorino cheese.
Serves 4

TV dinners are one of life's guilty pleasures.

split pea soup

3 tablespoons olive oil
3 leeks, white part only, chopped
4 garlic cloves, crushed
sea salt
freshly ground black pepper
500 g (1 lb 2 oz) dried green split peas,
  soaked overnight and drained
2 litres (70 fl oz/8 cups) chicken stock

to serve
3 tablespoons chopped fresh flat-leaf
  (Italian) parsley
toasted ham and cheese sandwiches,
  below

Heat a large saucepan over medium heat, add the olive oil, leeks and garlic and season with salt and pepper. Cook, stirring, until the leeks are translucent. Add the split peas and chicken stock, bring to the boil and then reduce the heat to low. Simmer for 40 minutes, stirring occasionally and skimming any froth from the top.

Ladle into serving bowls, sprinkle with parsley and serve with toasted ham and cheese sandwiches. Serves 4

toasted ham and cheese sandwiches

8 slices white sourdough bread
1 tablespoon dijon mustard
4 thick slices leg ham
4 slices gruyère or swiss-style cheese
sea salt
freshly ground black pepper
2 tablespoons olive oil

Spread four slices of bread with dijon mustard. Top with a slice of ham, then cheese, salt and pepper and another slice of bread to make a sandwich.

Heat a large non-stick frying pan over medium heat. Add half the olive oil and swirl to cover the base of the pan. Put two sandwiches in the pan and put another frying pan on top to squash them down. (I often put a couple of cans in the top frying pan for extra weight and this makes the sandwiches nice and crisp.) Cook for 1–2 minutes, until golden underneath, then flip them over, replace the weight and cook for a couple of minutes longer. Use the rest of the oil to cook the other two sandwiches. Serves 4

spicy pumpkin soup

1 tablespoon olive oil
1 red onion, sliced
2.5 cm (1 inch) piece of fresh ginger,
  sliced
2 teaspoons Thai red curry paste
1.6 kg (3 lb 8 oz) butternut pumpkin
  (squash), peeled, seeded and cubed
170 ml (5½ fl oz/⅔ cup) coconut milk
1 tablespoon fish sauce
1 tablespoon lime juice
1–2 teaspoons sugar, or to taste

to serve
small handful shredded fresh coriander
  (cilantro) leaves

Soup is always good to make in bulk
because it's so easy to freeze — just don't
add the coriander leaves until after you've
reheated or they will discolour.

Place a large saucepan over medium heat. Add the olive oil, onion, ginger and curry
paste and cook for 1 minute until fragrant. Add the pumpkin and stir to coat with the
paste. Add 1 litre (35 fl oz/4 cups) of water and bring to the boil. Reduce the heat and
simmer for 30 minutes or until the pumpkin is tender.

Transfer to a blender and mix until smooth. Return to the pan, stir in the coconut milk
and season with the fish sauce, lime juice and sugar. Heat through gently before
serving. Top with the coriander leaves. Serves 4

sausages with wholewheat fusilli

1 tablespoon olive oil
4 Italian-style sausages
1 red onion, cut into wedges
1 red capsicum (pepper), roughly
 chopped
2 garlic cloves, crushed
2 x 400 g (14 oz) tins chopped tomatoes
½ teaspoon dried red chilli flakes
1 teaspoon sugar
sea salt
2 tablespoons fresh oregano
500 g (1 lb 2 oz) wholewheat fusilli

Heat the oil in a saucepan or frying pan over medium–high heat and cook the
sausages for 6 minutes, turning occasionally. Lift out onto a plate, reduce the heat to
medium and cook the onion, capsicum and garlic for 4 minutes. Add the tomatoes,
chilli, sugar, salt and oregano and simmer for about 10 minutes or until the sauce has
thickened. Slice the sausages, return to the pan and heat through for 2 minutes.

Meanwhile, cook the pasta in a large saucepan of boiling salted water until *al dente*.
Drain well and top with the sauce. Serves 4

beef stroganoff with buttered noodles

2 rump steaks (about 800 g/1 lb 12 oz)
1–2 tablespoons olive oil
sea salt
freshly ground black pepper
2 tablespoons butter
1 large red onion, sliced into rings
2 garlic cloves, finely chopped
500 g (1 lb 2 oz) button mushrooms,
 sliced
2 teaspoons chopped fresh thyme
2 tablespoons tomato paste (purée)
2 tablespoons dijon mustard
185 ml (6 fl oz/¾ cup) crème fraîche

500 g (1 lb 2 oz) fettucine or wide
 noodles
2 tablespoons olive oil, extra

to serve
chopped fresh flat-leaf (Italian) parsley

Trim the fat and any sinew from the rump steaks and cut into thin strips. Heat a large heavy-based frying pan over high heat. Add 1 tablespoon of the oil and a handful of the steak strips, season with salt and pepper and brown all over. Remove to a warm plate as soon as the strips are sealed. Continue cooking in batches, adding extra oil as needed, until all the meat is sealed.

Add 1 tablespoon of the butter to the pan. Add the onion and garlic and cook until the onion is soft. Add the mushrooms and thyme and cook for 4 minutes until most of the liquid has evaporated. Add the tomato paste and cook for 1 minute. Return the sealed meat to the pan and stir in the mustard. Remove from the heat and fold in the crème fraîche.

Cook the pasta or noodles in a large saucepan of boiling salted water until *al dente* and then drain. Add the extra olive oil, remaining butter and salt and pepper and toss together. Divide the noodles among four serving plates and top with the beef stroganoff. Sprinkle with parsley. Serves 4

This was one of my favourites as a child.

baked meatballs with tomatoes

500 g (1 lb 2 oz) minced (ground) beef
  or pork and veal
1 small onion, grated
55 g (2 oz/⅔ cup) fresh white
  breadcrumbs
3 tablespoons chopped fresh flat-leaf
  (Italian) parsley
3 tablespoons chopped fresh coriander
  (cilantro) leaves
1 egg, lightly beaten
1 teaspoon ground cumin
1 teaspoon sweet paprika
2 red chillies, finely chopped
sea salt
freshly ground black pepper

3 tablespoons olive oil
2 x 400 g (14 oz) tins chopped tomatoes
½ teaspoon sugar

to serve
roast chilli potatoes, below

Preheat the oven to 220°C (425°F/Gas 7). Combine the meat, onion, breadcrumbs, parsley, coriander, egg, cumin, paprika, half of the chilli and plenty of salt and pepper in a large bowl. Mix gently with your hands, then shape into small balls (I find wetting my hands makes this easier).

Toss the meatballs gently in the oil in a roasting tin and bake for 10–15 minutes. Transfer them to a frying pan over medium heat and add the tomatoes, sugar, remaining chilli and some more salt and pepper. Stir the meatballs carefully to coat and then simmer for 20 minutes. Serve with the roast chilli potatoes. Serves 4–6

roast chilli potatoes

1 kg (2 lb 4 oz) potatoes, peeled and
  roughly diced
2 tablespoons olive oil
sea salt
1 long red chilli, thinly sliced
3 spring onions (scallions), thinly sliced
small handful chopped fresh coriander
  (cilantro) leaves

Preheat the oven to 220°C (425°F/Gas 7). Toss the potatoes with the olive oil, place on a large baking tray and season with sea salt. Roast for 40 minutes, turning once, until golden and crispy. Scatter with the chilli, spring onions and coriander leaves and return to the oven for another 2 minutes before serving. Serves 4–6

cheat's porcini risotto

10 g (¼ oz) packet dried porcini
  mushrooms
1 tablespoon olive oil
1 white onion, finely chopped
sea salt
25 g (1 oz) butter
250 g (9 oz) arborio rice
500 ml (17 fl oz/2 cups) chicken stock
50 g (1¾ oz/½ cup) grated parmesan
  cheese
freshly ground black pepper

to serve
3 tablespoons shredded fresh flat-leaf
  (Italian) parsley
2 tablespoons grated parmesan cheese

My favourite Italian cook, Marcella Hazan, says to look for large porcini with a predominantly creamy colour and to avoid packets with small, dark, crumbly pieces of mushroom. If your mushrooms are gritty, rinse them clean under cold running water before you soak them. Marcella also suggests filtering the porcini soaking water if you can see dirt at the bottom of the bowl — simply pour it through a sieve lined with either muslin or paper towel.

First, reconstitute the porcini mushrooms by soaking them in 500 ml (17 fl oz/2 cups) of luke-warm water for 30 minutes.

Heat a large heavy-based saucepan and add the oil, onion, salt and half the butter. Cook over low heat until the onion is translucent but not browned, stirring occasionally. Add the rice and stir for a few minutes until the grains are glistening. Increase the heat to high and add the porcini mushrooms, soaking water and chicken stock and bring to the boil. Cover the pan and reduce the heat to a simmer. Cook for 15 minutes, stirring occasionally. Remove from the heat and stir in the parmesan, remaining butter and black pepper. Serve sprinkled with parsley and parmesan.
Serves 2

Some people find stirring risotto relaxing — I'm not one of them!

I like to serve this with parmesan roast potatoes. Peel and quarter 800 g (1 lb 12 oz) potatoes and boil until tender. Toss them with 3 tablespoons of olive oil, some sea salt, black pepper and 50 g (1³/₄ oz/ ¹/₂ cup) of grated parmesan. Put in a baking tin and roast for 30 minutes at 220°C (425°F/Gas 7). Shake the tin occasionally so the potatoes don't stick.

crispy chicken and cavalo nero with garlic and chilli

4 boneless chicken thighs, with skin
1 tablespoon olive oil, plus 1 teaspoon
  extra
sea salt
freshly ground black pepper
1 garlic clove, sliced
½ long red chilli, roughly chopped
1 teaspoon lemon zest
1 tablespoon lemon juice
300 g (10½ oz) cavalo nero, trimmed

to serve
lemon wedges
parmesan roast potatoes, left

Heat a frying pan over medium heat. Toss the chicken with 1 tablespoon of the oil, salt and pepper and put in the pan. Put another frying pan on top to squash the chicken down (I often put a couple of cans in the top frying pan for extra weight to make the chicken really crisp) and cook for 3–4 minutes on each side, until cooked through. Lift out of the pan and set aside.

Reheat the frying pan over medium–high heat. Add the extra oil and the garlic, chilli and lemon zest and cook for 1 minute or until golden. Add the lemon juice and cavalo nero and cook for 2 minutes or until just wilted. Serve the cavalo nero with the crispy chicken, lemon wedges and parmesan roast potatoes. Serves 2

Buy good-quality fresh lasagne (you'll need about 12 sheets). You don't need to soak or precook them; just trim them to fit the size of your lasagne dish.

ham lasagne

3 x 400 g (14 oz) tins chopped tomatoes
500 g (1 lb 2 oz) cherry tomatoes
3 garlic cloves, crushed
2 tablespoons olive oil
sea salt
600 g (1 lb 5 oz) fresh lasagne
12 thick slices leg ham
750 g (1 lb 10 oz/3 cups) fresh ricotta
450 g (1 lb) fresh mozzarella or
  bocconcini (baby mozzarella), sliced
100 g (3½ oz) parmesan cheese, grated
freshly ground black pepper
1 tablespoon olive oil, extra

to serve
small handful fresh basil leaves

Preheat the oven to 180°C (350°F/Gas 4). Empty the tins of tomatoes into a saucepan with the cherry tomatoes and bring to the boil. Reduce the heat to low and simmer for 20–25 minutes. Add the garlic, olive oil and a generous pinch of salt and cook for another minute.

Cut the lasagne sheets to fit a 25 x 35 cm (10 x 14 inch) ovenproof dish. Lightly grease the dish with olive oil and spread with three tablespoons of the tomato sauce. Top with a sheet of pasta and then an eighth of the tomato sauce. Tear and scatter an eighth each of the ham, ricotta and mozzarella over the sauce. Repeat the layers until the pasta, sauce, ham and cheese have been used up. Sprinkle parmesan, salt and pepper over the top and drizzle with the extra olive oil.

Cover the lasagne with foil and bake for 20 minutes. Remove the foil and bake for another 30 minutes or until brown. Scatter with basil leaves to serve. Serves 6

I always make a couple of these. One for now and one for the freezer.

I like to roll my limes on the bench, pressing firmly, before squeezing. This way they give out maximum juice.

red curry fish with sweet potato

2 tablespoons light-flavoured oil (I like canola)
1 onion, sliced
2 garlic cloves, sliced
2 tablespoons Thai red curry paste
375 ml (13 fl oz/1½ cups) chicken stock
125 ml (4 fl oz/½ cup) coconut milk
350 g (12 oz) orange sweet potato, peeled and diced
200 g (7 oz) snake (yard-long) beans, trimmed and cut into long lengths
750 g (1 lb 10 oz) firm white fish (I like cod or snapper), cut into large pieces
200 g (7 oz) cherry tomatoes
3 tablespoons lime juice
1 tablespoon fish sauce

to serve
coriander (cilantro) leaves
steamed rice

Heat a saucepan over high heat. Add the oil and stir-fry the onion for 2 minutes. Add the garlic and cook for 1 minute. Add the curry paste and cook for another minute or until fragrant.

Add the stock, coconut milk and sweet potato and bring to a simmer. Cook for 15–20 minutes or until tender. Add the beans, fish and cherry tomatoes, cover the pan and simmer gently for 5 minutes until the fish is just cooked. Stir through the lime juice and fish sauce and sprinkle with coriander leaves. Serve with steamed rice. Serves 4

rigatoni with fresh olive puttanesca

500 g (1 lb 2 oz) rigatoni
2 tablespoons olive oil
10 anchovies, chopped
1 red chilli, chopped, optional
½ red onion, finely sliced
250 g (9 oz) yellow teardrop tomatoes,
  halved
3 tablespoons salted capers, rinsed
20 green olives, halved and pitted
2 tablespoons red wine vinegar
sea salt
freshly ground black pepper

to serve
small handful torn fresh basil leaves

Cook the pasta in a large saucepan of boiling salted water until *al dente*. While the pasta is cooking, put the oil, anchovies and chilli in a bowl and place it over the pasta pan to heat gently.

Drain the pasta and toss with the onion, tomatoes, capers, olives, vinegar, salt, pepper and anchovy mixture. Scatter with basil leaves to serve. Serves 4

For me, dried pasta works well with light summery flavours while fresh pasta stands up to heartier sauces.

bistecca alla pizzaiola

2 T-bone steaks, 2 cm (¾ inch) thick
extra virgin olive oil, for brushing
sea salt
freshly ground black pepper
125 ml (4 fl oz/½ cup) white wine
250 ml (9 fl oz/1 cup) good-quality
  tomato pasta sauce
¼ teaspoon dried red chilli flakes
1 tablespoon fresh oregano

to serve
1 tablespoon chopped fresh flat-leaf
  (Italian) parsley
crispy potatoes, below

Heat a large frying pan over high heat. Brush both sides of the steak with olive oil and season well with salt and pepper. Cook the steak for 1 minute on each side until brown, then remove from the pan and set aside. Add the wine to the hot pan and stir for 1 minute to reduce slightly. Stir in the tomato sauce, chilli and oregano.

Put the steak back in the pan, reduce the heat to medium and cook for 5 minutes, turning once. Sprinkle with parsley and serve with crispy potatoes. Serves 2

crispy potatoes

6 small new potatoes
sea salt
3 tablespoons grated parmesan cheese
2 tablespoons olive oil
freshly ground black pepper
1 teaspoon lemon zest
1 garlic clove, crushed

Preheat the oven to 220°C (425°F/Gas 7). Boil the potatoes in salted water for about 15 minutes until tender. Drain and leave to cool slightly.

Put the potatoes on a baking tray and flatten with the palm of your hand (or a fork or potato masher). Mix together the parmesan, olive oil, salt, pepper, lemon zest and garlic and sprinkle over the potatoes. Bake for 25 minutes until crispy. Serves 2

The crispy potatoes are inspired by one of my favourite cooks, Jill Dupleix.

chicken with paprika and chorizo

1 x 1.6 kg (3 lb 8 oz) chicken, cut into
   8 pieces
sea salt
freshly ground black pepper
1 teaspoon paprika
1 tablespoon olive oil
2 chorizo sausages, sliced
2 onions, thinly sliced
2 red capsicums (peppers), cut into
   strips
2 green capsicums (peppers), cut into
   strips
6 garlic cloves, finely sliced
500 ml (17 fl oz/2 cups) chicken stock
400 g (14 oz) tin chopped tomatoes
1 tablespoon tomato paste (purée)

to serve
rice with broad beans, below

Pimento is Spanish paprika. The Spanish
'pimenton de la vera' is smoked paprika
with a sweet, woody, smoky bacon flavour
that is fabulous with chicken, seafood or
potatoes. If you can't find it, just use
ordinary sweet paprika.

Season the chicken liberally with salt and pepper and toss to coat with the paprika.
Heat a large casserole dish, add the oil and cook the chorizo until crisp. Remove the
chorizo and brown the chicken in two batches for 5 minutes on each side. Lift out the
chicken, pour away any excess oil and put the casserole back over high heat.

Add the onion, sprinkle with salt and cook for 5 minutes. Add the capsicum and garlic
and cook for 10 minutes longer, stirring occasionally. Put the chicken on top of the
capsicum and pour the combined stock, tomatoes and tomato paste over the top.
Simmer for 20 minutes over medium–low heat, stirring occasionally.

Remove the chicken pieces and bring the liquid to the boil. Boil for 10–15 minutes
to thicken the sauce, then return the chicken and chorizo to the casserole to heat
through. Serve with rice with broad beans. Serves 4

rice with broad beans

400 g (14 oz/2 cups) long-grain rice
1 lemon, cut in half
350 g (12 oz/2 cups) broad (fava) beans,
   blanched and peeled, or peas

sea salt
1 tablespoon chopped fresh flat-leaf
   (Italian) parsley

Bring a large saucepan of water to the boil over high heat. Add the rice and lemon
and cook for 15 minutes, stirring occasionally. Drain and return the rice to the pan
with the beans. Season with salt and stir in the parsley. Cover the pan until you are
ready to serve (I find it will keep like this for about 20 minutes). Serves 4

apple and passionfruit crumble

6 granny smith apples, peeled and
  thinly sliced
110 g (3¾ oz/½ cup) sugar
pulp from 8 passionfruit

topping
130 g (4½ oz/1 cup) rolled oats
125 g (4½ oz/⅔ cup) soft brown sugar
40 g (1½ oz/⅓ cup) plain (all-purpose)
  flour
100 g (3½ oz) butter, softened

to serve
vanilla ice cream or thick (double/heavy)
  cream

Preheat the oven to 180°C (350°F/Gas 4) and grease a 2 litre (70 fl oz/8 cup) baking dish. Mix together the apples, sugar and passionfruit pulp and put in the dish.

With your hands, rub together the oats, brown sugar, flour and butter to make a crumbly topping. Sprinkle over the fruit and bake for 25–30 minutes until golden. Serve with ice cream or cream. Serves 4

banana butterscotch pudding

125 g (4½ oz/1 cup) plain (all-purpose)
  flour
pinch of salt
115 g (4 oz/½ cup) caster (superfine)
  sugar
3 teaspoons baking powder
1 banana, mashed
250 ml (9 fl oz/1 cup) milk
85 g (3 oz) unsalted butter, melted
1 egg, lightly beaten
1 teaspoon natural vanilla extract

topping
140 g (5 oz/¾ cup) soft brown sugar
3 tablespoons golden syrup

to serve
vanilla ice cream or thick (double/heavy)
  cream

Preheat the oven to 180°C (350°F/Gas 4). Sift the flour, salt, sugar and baking
powder into a bowl. Add the banana, milk, butter, egg and vanilla and whisk together
well. Pour into a greased 2 litre (70 fl oz/8 cup) baking dish and put the dish on a
baking tray.

To make the topping, put the brown sugar, golden syrup and 250 ml (9 fl oz/1 cup)
of boiling water in a small saucepan and bring to the boil. Pour carefully over the
pudding, then bake for 30–40 minutes or until cooked through when tested with a
skewer. Serve with vanilla ice cream or cream. Serves 4

The flavours of this old-fashioned pudding are
surprisingly good after Asian food.

caramel pecan sundae

185 g (6½ oz/1 cup) soft brown sugar
250 ml (9 fl oz/1 cup) cream
1 teaspoon natural vanilla extract
20 g (¾ oz) unsalted butter

to serve
vanilla ice cream
toasted pecans

Put the sugar, cream, vanilla and butter in a small pan over medium heat. Stir well and bring to a gentle boil. Cook, stirring occasionally, for 10 minutes or until thick and syrupy. Leave to cool a little and then pour over ice cream in bowls and top with toasted pecans. Serves 6

This is the sort of thing I make at nine o'clock in the evening when the kids are in bed.

lazy days

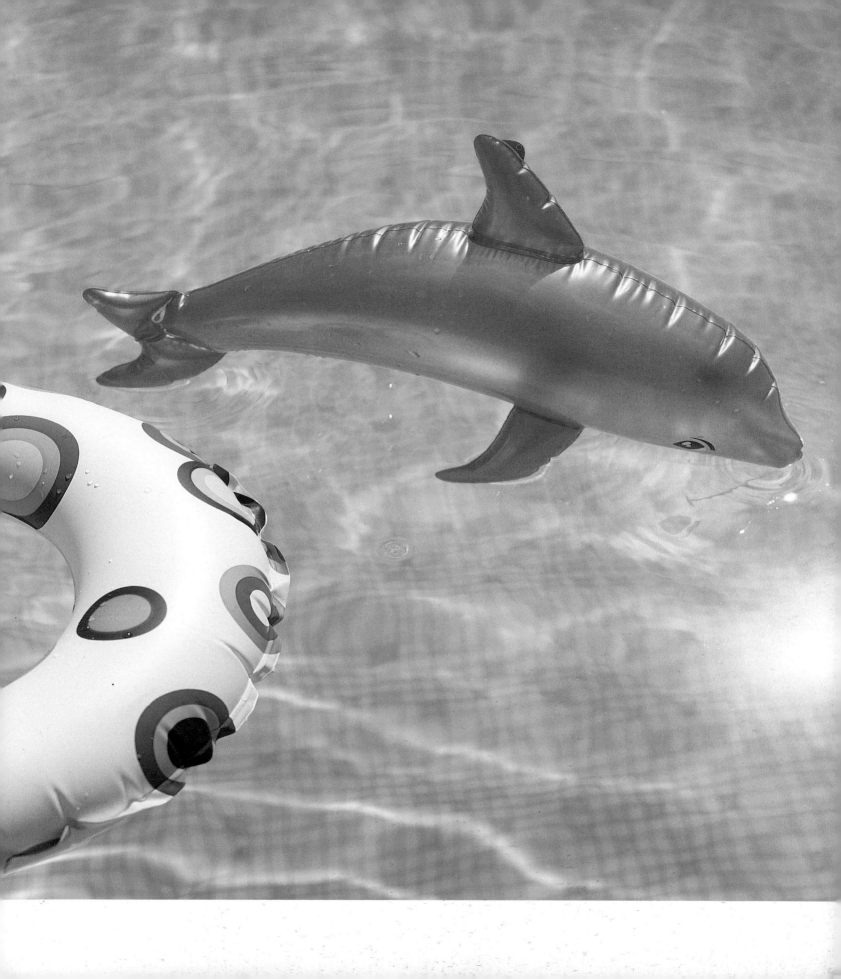

I really love inviting friends to our home. But there are occasional times when I've asked people over and things have gone pear-shaped with the preparations or I just feel like kicking back with a glass of wine and some good conversation instead of heading to the kitchen. Entertaining can be very easy if you mix a few recipes you make from scratch with a selection of bought food. It can be much quicker, and far less stress, especially if you've not much time or energy to spare. So, if 'cheating' by buying a few bits and pieces means you get to spend more time chatting with your friends and family, then why not?

indian not-completely-take-away

From your favourite Indian restaurant, buy pieces of tandoori chicken, basmati rice, naan bread and, if they make them, Indian sweets. Bring out the mango chutney and then all you need to make is spinach raita, dhal and a simple tomato salad.

Not many people think of serving Indian sweets so they're an unusual way to finish off a meal. Try little squares of carrot halva, burfi with pistachio and jalebi.

spinach raita

350 g (12 oz) English spinach, trimmed
500 g (1 lb 2 oz/2 cups) plain yoghurt
2 garlic cloves, crushed
sea salt
freshly ground black pepper

Wash the spinach and put in a pan over medium heat with just the water clinging to the leaves. Cover and cook for 3–5 minutes until wilted, stirring occasionally. Drain and squeeze out the water. Whisk together the yoghurt, garlic, salt and pepper until smooth. Stir in the spinach and refrigerate until required. Serves 4–6

tomato salad with lime

500 g (1 lb 2 oz) cherry tomatoes,
  halved
1–2 green chillies, finely chopped
2 garlic cloves, crushed
1 tablespoon lime juice
¼ teaspoon sea salt
½ teaspoon sugar

Gently stir together all the ingredients. Serves 4–6

If you like your dhal mild, remove the seeds from the chilli. If you prefer your food hot and spicy, leave them in.

my dhal

2 tablespoons olive oil
1 red onion, finely sliced
2.5 cm (1 inch) piece of fresh ginger, peeled and grated
3 garlic cloves, finely sliced
1 large green chilli, finely chopped
1 teaspoon sea salt
1 teaspoon ground cumin
250 g (9 oz/1 cup) red lentils
1 tablespoon lime juice

to serve
small handful fresh coriander (cilantro) leaves
naan bread

Heat a heavy-based saucepan over medium heat and add the olive oil. When hot, add the onion, ginger, garlic, chilli, salt and cumin and cook for 10 minutes, stirring occasionally, until the onion is soft. Add the lentils and 750 ml (26 fl oz/3 cups) of water and cook, stirring occasionally, for 20 minutes until the lentils have dissolved.

Remove from the heat and stir through the lime juice. Top with the coriander leaves and serve with naan bread. Serves 4–6

Pulses are a favourite food of mine. Just remember they need lots of seasoning.

new york deli brunch

Buy a bag of fresh bagels and spread them with cream cheese (perhaps whipped with lemon juice, capers or chives), smoked salmon and a red onion and parsley salad. Fold thin slices of pastrami, swiss cheese and dill pickle on rye bread to make open sandwiches. Make a pot of the best plunger coffee and produce a spectacular upside-down plum cake that you've baked yourself.

red onion and parsley salad

1 red onion, thinly sliced
1 tablespoon salted capers, rinsed
small handful chopped fresh flat-leaf
  (Italian) parsley
3 tablespoons lemon juice
sea salt

to serve
cream cheese
smoked salmon
bagels

Toss together all the ingredients and serve with cream cheese, smoked salmon and bagels. Makes enough to fill 6 bagels

It's a bit of a myth that you should leave coffee to stand before plunging. Pour the almost-boiling water over the coffee, stir and slowly plunge straightaway to extract the flavour (just like an espresso machine).

upside-down plum cake

850 g (1 lb 14 oz) plums
50 g (1¾ oz) unsalted butter, softened
115 g (4 oz/½ cup) caster (superfine)
  sugar
1 tablespoon lemon juice

cake
100 g (3½ oz) unsalted butter
225 g (8 oz/1 cup) caster (superfine)
  sugar
4 eggs, separated
1 teaspoon natural vanilla extract
155 g (5½ oz/1¼ cups) plain
  (all-purpose) flour
2 teaspoons baking powder
1 teaspoon ground cinnamon
pinch of salt

to serve
cream or crème fraîche

Preheat the oven to 180°C (350°F/Gas 4). Use a sharp knife to slice the cheeks from the plums and discard the stones. To make the caramel, melt the butter in an ovenproof 28 cm (11 inch) frying pan over low heat. Add the sugar and lemon juice and stir until dissolved. Increase the heat and cook for 5–6 minutes, or until golden and caramelized. Transfer the plums to the pan and cook gently for 2 minutes.

To make the cake, cream together the butter and sugar until light and fluffy. Add the egg yolks, one at a time, beating well after each addition, then add the vanilla extract. Sift the flour, baking powder, cinnamon and salt over the mixture and beat until smooth. Beat the egg whites in a clean dry bowl until stiff. Fold into the mixture with a metal spoon. Spoon over the plums in the pan, smoothing the surface with a spatula.

Bake for 40 minutes, or until a skewer inserted into the centre comes out clean. Leave to rest for a minute before carefully turning out and serving with cream or crème fraîche. Serves 10–12

I always love a picnic — although we don't usually get any further than the backyard.

Pomegranate molasses is a treacly-thick dark-brown sauce made by boiling down pomegranate juice. It has a rich acidic flavour that works well in dressings or marinades. Buy it at Middle-Eastern delis.

mezze picnic

Lebanese mezze is perfectly portable for an outdoor feast. Buy marinated olives and pitta bread. Fry slices of haloumi cheese and sprinkle with chopped chilli and lemon juice. Make easy hummus, tabbouleh and silverbeet rolls (or, if you're really short for time, buy dolmades) and bring out Turkish delight to finish.

tabbouleh

60 g (2¼ oz/⅓ cup) cracked wheat
2 tomatoes, chopped
1 Lebanese cucumber, chopped
4 spring onions (scallions), sliced
large handful roughly chopped fresh
  flat-leaf (Italian) parsley
large handful roughly chopped
  fresh mint
2 tablespoons extra virgin olive oil
1 tablespoon lemon juice
1 tablespoon pomegranate molasses
sea salt

Soak the cracked wheat in 125 ml (4 fl oz/½ cup) of water until soft. Toss together the tomato, cucumber, spring onion, parsley, mint and wheat in a bowl. Add the olive oil, lemon juice, pomegranate molasses and salt and stir through before serving.
Serves 4

silverbeet rolls

2 bunches silverbeet (Swiss chard)
sea salt
1 tablespoon lemon juice

filling
180 g (6½ oz/1 cup) drained tinned
    chickpeas
200 g (7 oz/1 cup) long-grain rice
250 g (9 oz/1 cup) tinned chopped
    tomatoes
2 red onions, finely diced
1½ teaspoons ground cumin

1 teaspoon paprika
small handful chopped fresh parsley
sea salt
freshly ground black pepper
1 long red chilli, finely diced
2 tablespoons finely chopped fresh mint

to serve
olive oil
lemon wedges

I love to serve Turkish delight after a mezze platter. It's a gorgeously easy dessert that looks really pretty in a bowl. There's a variety of different flavours — I'm particularly partial to the hazelnut.

Wash the silverbeet thoroughly and then cut away the stalks and centre stems. Cut the leaves into 10 cm (4 inch) squares, keeping the leftover scraps. Line a deep frying pan with the leftover pieces of silverbeet. Put the silverbeet squares in a bowl of boiling water to soften them. Refresh under cold water and drain in a colander.

To make filling, stir together all the filling ingredients. Take a piece of silverbeet, making sure it is not broken, and place 1 tablespoon of filling in the centre. Roll up the silverbeet square halfway, fold in the edges and then roll up completely.

Put the rolls in the lined frying pan in tightly packed rows. Pour the salt, lemon juice and 125 ml (4 fl oz/½ cup) of water over the top. Cover the pan and bring to the boil. Reduce the heat to medium and cook for 20–30 minutes (check that the pan isn't drying out: you can add a little more water if necessary). Drizzle with a little olive oil and serve with lemon wedges. Makes about 35

easy hummus

440 g (14 oz/2 cups) drained tinned
    chickpeas
½ teaspoon ground cumin
2 tablespoons chopped fresh coriander
    (cilantro) leaves
2 tablespoons lemon juice
sea salt
freshly ground black pepper
1 tablespoon tahini (optional)

to serve
1 tablespoon extra virgin olive oil
coriander (cilantro) leaves

Put all the ingredients in a blender with 3 tablespoons of warm water and mix until smooth. Drizzle with olive oil and scatter with coriander leaves to serve. Serves 4

antipasto lunch

Italian antipasto is almost as simple to make as it is to buy. Roasted capsicums (peppers) are delicious with anchovies, capers and fresh oregano. Slice figs and serve with prosciutto and a drizzle of extra virgin olive oil. And buy a selection of wonderful Italian nougat. All that remains to make is a couple of salads and my friend Giovanni's sausages and potatoes.

zucchini and parmesan salad

2 yellow zucchini (courgettes)
2 green zucchini (courgettes)
2 tablespoons lemon juice
30 g (1 oz) parmesan cheese shavings
1 tablespoon extra virgin olive oil
freshly ground black pepper
sea salt

Slice the zucchini lengthways as thinly as you can (use a mandolin if you have one). Put in a bowl with the lemon juice, stir together and leave to marinate for 20 minutes. Toss with the parmesan, drizzle with the olive oil and season with salt and pepper before serving. Serves 4

giovanni's sausages with potatoes and rosemary

6 Italian-style sausages
800 g (1 lb 12 oz) potatoes, scrubbed
  and sliced (I use kipfler/fingerling)
1½ teaspoons paprika
2 rosemary stalks
sea salt
freshly ground black pepper
½ loaf ciabatta, crust removed
50 ml (1¾ fl oz) extra virgin olive oil

to serve
handful fresh basil leaves
rocket (arugula) leaves

Preheat the oven to 200°C (400°F/Gas 6). Slice the sausages thickly and place in a large roasting tin. Add the potatoes, paprika, rosemary, sea salt and pepper. Tear the ciabatta into bite-size pieces and add to the tin. Drizzle with the oil and toss gently.

Roast, stirring occasionally, for 30–40 minutes or until the potatoes are tender and the sausages and bread are golden brown. Sprinkle with the basil and serve with a salad of rocket leaves. Serves 4

shredded radicchio salad

2 radicchio, shredded
4 tablespoons extra virgin olive oil
1½ tablespoons orange juice
pinch of sugar

Put the radicchio in a bowl. Mix together the oil, orange juice and sugar and toss with the radicchio. Serves 4

You can pick up real nougat from a good deli instead of making dessert at home.

When you're squeezing fresh fruit for juices, try combining two or three. Grapefruit and passionfruit is a personal favourite.

sunday brunch

Brunch requires little more than a visit to your favourite deli, bakery and fruit shop. You need a loaf of sourdough or rye bread, a generous wedge of gruyère cheese, ham thickly sliced from the bone and a jug of freshly squeezed blood orange juice or grapefruit and passionfruit juice. Make a fragrant tomato and basil salad and a hot batch of berry muffins. Just before your guests arrive, cut a platter of the most perfect fruit in season.

tomato and basil salad

5 ripe tomatoes, at room temperature
sea salt
2 tablespoons extra virgin olive oil
small handful fresh basil leaves

Slice the tomatoes and arrange on a platter. Sprinkle with sea salt, drizzle with the extra virgin olive oil and sprinkle with basil leaves to serve. Serves 6

triple berry muffins

120 g (4¼ oz) unsalted butter, at room
  temperature
225 g (8 oz/1 cup) caster (superfine)
  sugar
2 eggs
1½ teaspoons natural vanilla extract
170 ml (5½ fl oz/⅔ cup) sour cream
210 g (7½ oz/1⅔ cups) self-raising flour
1¼ teaspoons baking powder
sea salt
150 g (5½ oz) mixed berries

Preheat the oven to 180ºC (350ºF/Gas 4). Line twelve 125 ml (4 fl oz/½ cup) muffin holes with paper muffin cases.

Cream together the butter and sugar until light and fluffy. Add the eggs, one at a time, mixing well after each addition, then add the vanilla and sour cream and mix well. Sift in the flour, baking powder and a pinch of salt and mix until almost combined. Add the berries and gently fold through the mixture. Spoon into the muffin cases and bake for 25 minutes until golden. Makes 12

You can use fresh or frozen berries here. When the mixture is almost combined, fold in the berries very gently with a large metal spoon. Try to avoid breaking them up or they will bleed through the rest of the mixture. If you toss the berries with a little flour first, they won't sink in the muffins.

little days

I'm not really a fan of making special meals for children. I always give the girls food that we like to eat, for purely selfish reasons: like most parents I don't want to cook twice in an evening. But sometimes it's good to get the kids fed early, so I do have a few stand-bys for very simple kiddy dinners — and I admit that sometimes these become our dinner as well! I try to keep meals as pure and balanced as possible, serving a range of different foods. If you find your kids don't eat something, keep serving it and don't make a big deal about it. Spoil your family with fresh food, not processed treats. Forget designer clothes or expensive toys — the most important gift we can give our children is a palate for good unadulterated food, which in turn can lead to a long healthy life.

rigatoni and chicken bolognese

2 tablespoons extra virgin olive oil
1 onion, chopped
1 celery stalk, finely chopped
2 garlic cloves, chopped
sea salt
freshly ground black pepper
2 slices pancetta or prosciutto, chopped
500 g (1 lb 2 oz) minced (ground)
  chicken
375 ml (13 fl oz/1½ cups) tomato
  passata (puréed tomatoes)
500 g (1 lb 2 oz) rigatoni

to serve
3 tablespoons chopped fresh flat-leaf
  (Italian) parsley
grated parmesan cheese

Put the oil, onion, celery, garlic and a good pinch of salt and pepper in a saucepan over medium heat and cook for about 7 minutes until golden. Add the pancetta and chicken and stir constantly with a wooden spoon to break up any lumps. When the mince is cooked through, add the passata and simmer for 10 minutes.

Meanwhile, cook the pasta in a large saucepan of boiling salted water until *al dente*. Drain and toss with the sauce. To serve, fold in the parsley and top with grated parmesan. Serves 4 adults or lots of children

If your children have a real aversion to 'greenery', leave out the parsley for now.

I don't know how we ever lived without pasta — it's such a quick and easy food to have in the pantry when you're feeding children. Buy a variety of shapes to keep them interested at dinnertime, and don't forget to always add some protein (a meat sauce, cheese, or pesto with pine nuts) to make it a complete meal.

pasta bows with spring peas and prosciutto

1 tablespoon extra virgin olive oil
100 g (3½ oz) prosciutto, sliced
1 white onion, sliced
250 ml (9 fl oz/1 cup) chicken stock
200 g (7 oz) shelled fresh peas
500 g (1 lb 2 oz) farfalle
1 tablespoon butter
250 g (9 oz/1 cup) fresh ricotta
sea salt
freshly ground black pepper

Place a saucepan over low heat and add the oil. Cook the prosciutto until golden, then remove from the pan. Add the onion to the pan and cook until soft. Add the stock and bring to the boil. Cook until the stock has reduced by half, then add the peas and simmer gently for 3 minutes.

Cook the pasta in a large saucepan of boiling salted water until *al dente*. Drain well and add to the sauce with the butter. To serve, spoon into two bowls, crumble the ricotta over the top and season with salt and pepper. Serves 2 adults or 4 children

too-tired-to-cook pasta with cheese

500 g (1 lb 2 oz) pasta wheels
50 g (1¾ oz) butter
50 g (1¾ oz/½ cup) grated parmesan
  cheese
sea salt

to serve
grated parmesan cheese
2 tablespoons fresh basil leaves

Cook the pasta in a large saucepan of boiling salted water until *al dente*. Drain well and return to the warm pan. Stir in the butter and parmesan and sprinkle with sea salt. Serve topped with extra parmesan and the basil. Serves 4 adults or lots of children

fish fingers with parmesan crust

80 g (2¾ oz/1 cup) fresh breadcrumbs
50 g (1¾ oz/½ cup) grated parmesan
  cheese
sea salt
freshly ground black pepper
2 eggs, lightly beaten
60 g (2¼ oz/½ cup) plain (all-purpose)
  flour
500 g (1 lb 2 oz) firm white fish fillets
  (I like flathead), cut into fat strips
1 tablespoon olive oil
25 g (1 oz) butter

to serve
lemon wedges
oven-baked fries, below
caper mayonnaise, right

Fish fingers, whether they're for kids or adults, are always great with caper mayonnaise. Just stir a few capers, some lemon juice and chopped flat-leaf (Italian) parsley through whole-egg mayonnaise.

Mix together the breadcrumbs, parmesan, salt and pepper in a bowl. Put the eggs in another bowl. Mix the flour with salt and pepper in a third bowl. Dip each piece of fish in the flour, then the egg, then the breadcrumbs. (You can do this in advance if you like, and then keep the crumbed fish covered in the fridge for up to 2 hours.)

Heat the olive oil and butter in a large non-stick frying pan over medium–high heat. Add the fish in batches and cook gently for about 2 minutes on each side, until lightly golden, adding a little more oil and butter if it is needed. Serve with fries and lemon wedges, and perhaps a bowl of caper mayonnaise. Serves 4 adults or lots of children

oven-baked fries

1.25 kg (2 lb 12 oz) potatoes, scrubbed
  but not peeled
3 teaspoons olive oil
sea salt

Preheat the oven to 230°C (450°F/Gas 8) and put two baking trays in the oven to heat up for 20 minutes. Cut the potatoes into chips, dry with a tea towel, toss with the oil and sprinkle with salt. Put the chips on baking paper on top of the hot baking trays and bake for 30 minutes or until golden, turning with tongs halfway through the cooking time. Serves 4 adults or lots of children

no-stir tomato risotto

1 tablespoon olive oil
25 g (1 oz) butter
1 onion, finely chopped
sea salt
250 g (9 oz) arborio rice
500 ml (17 fl oz/2 cups) chicken stock
250 ml (9 fl oz/1 cup) tomato passata
  (puréed tomatoes)
1 teaspoon sugar
2 tablespoons shredded fresh basil

Heat a large heavy-based saucepan over medium heat and add the oil, butter, onion and salt. Cook until the onion is translucent, stirring occasionally. Add the rice and stir for a few minutes until the grains are glistening. Increase the heat to high and add the stock, tomato passata and 375 ml (13 fl oz/1½ cups) of boiling water. Bring to the boil, stirring occasionally. Reduce the heat to low, cover and cook for 15–20 minutes.

Remove from the heat, stir in the sugar and scatter with the basil. Serves 4 adults or lots of children

There's no better, or easier, dessert for kids than a bowl of fresh berries.

stir-fried noodles with beef and sugar snaps

3 tablespoons oyster sauce
2 tablespoons soy sauce
1½ tablespoons dry sherry
3 tablespoons chicken stock
2 teaspoons sugar
1 tablespoon light-flavoured oil (I like canola)
400 g (14 oz) beef fillet or rump, sliced
4 cm (1½ inch) piece of fresh ginger, julienned or grated
200 g (7 oz) sugar snap peas

to serve
250 g (9 oz) fresh egg noodles, cooked and drained

Stir together the oyster sauce, soy sauce, sherry, stock and sugar in a small bowl.

Heat a wok or large frying pan over high heat. Add the oil and, when smoking, stir-fry the beef in two batches, cooking for 1 minute until it is sealed and browned. Remove from the wok and set aside. Stir-fry the ginger and peas for 2 minutes, adding a little more oil if needed. Add the beef and sauce and cook for 1 minute, until the sauce has thickened slightly.

Divide the noodles among four bowls and top with the stir-fry. (Or add the noodles to the wok and mix it all together.) Serves 4 adults or lots of children

Although it's expensive, beef fillet is great for children because it's so tender and you only need a little.

Children can really be involved with
making these biscuits. There's a lot of
rolling, pressing and spooning jam that
doesn't need much precision and is great
for small helping hands.

jam buttons

250 g (9 oz) unsalted butter, softened
3 tablespoons caster (superfine) sugar
zest of 1 orange
1 egg yolk
1 teaspoon natural vanilla extract
250 g (9 oz/2 cups) plain (all-purpose)
  flour, sifted
90 g (3¼ oz/1 cup) desiccated coconut
1½ tablespoons raspberry jam
1½ tablespoons apricot jam

Preheat the oven to 180°C (350°F/Gas 4). Line a large tray with baking paper.

Beat the butter, sugar and orange zest with electric beaters until pale. Add the
egg yolk and vanilla and beat until combined. Fold in the flour and coconut.

Roll tablespoon measures of the dough into balls, arrange on a baking tray about
2 cm (about 1 inch) apart and press to flatten slightly. Make an indent in the centre of
each one with your thumb. Place half a teaspoon of either jam in each indent. Bake
for 10–12 minutes or until lightly browned. Leave to cool on a wire rack. Makes 25–30

berry butterfly cakes

185 g (6½ oz/1½ cups) plain
  (all-purpose) flour
3 teaspoons baking powder
125 g (4½ oz) unsalted butter, softened
1 teaspoon natural vanilla extract
145 g (5 oz/⅔ cup) caster (superfine)
  sugar
2 eggs
125 ml (4 fl oz/½ cup) milk

to serve
freshly whipped cream
strawberries and raspberries
icing (confectioners') sugar

Preheat the oven to 180°C (350ºF/Gas 4). Sift the flour and baking powder into a bowl. Add the butter, vanilla, sugar, eggs and milk and mix, either with electric beaters or a wooden spoon, until smooth.

Arrange large cupcake cases in a 12-hole muffin tin and spoon the mixture into the cases. Bake for 17–20 minutes or until golden brown. Leave in the tin for 5 minutes before turning out onto a wire rack to cool.

Slice the tops off the cupcakes and cut each top in half. Spoon cream onto the cakes and decorate with strawberries and raspberries. Place the tops back on and sprinkle with icing sugar. Makes 12

While electric beaters are great time-savers, I always try to whip cream by hand. It gives me a little more control over the cream and prevents over-beating.

Get the kids involved in making the party food.
The preparation should be half the fun.

pitta pizza

easy sausage rolls with tomato sauce

500 ml (17 fl oz/2 cups) tomato passata
  (puréed tomatoes)
3 tablespoons soft brown sugar
2 teaspoons worcestershire sauce
1 tablespoon red wine vinegar
4 sheets puff pastry
10 thick sausages (about 1 kg/2 lb 4 oz)
2 egg yolks
2 tablespoons milk
sesame seeds

To make the sauce, put the passata, sugar, worcestershire sauce and vinegar in a
small pan over medium heat. Simmer for 10 minutes until thickened.

Preheat the oven to 200°C (400°F/Gas 6). Put the pastry on a board and cut the
sheets in half. Squeeze the sausage meat out of its casings along one long side of
the pastry. Mix the egg yolks and milk and brush along the outside edge of the pastry,
then roll up and cut each roll into three pieces. Place on a greased baking tray, with
the sealed edges underneath. Brush with more egg yolk and sprinkle with sesame
seeds. Bake for 20–25 minutes or until golden. Serve with the sauce. Makes 24

pitta pizza

1 pitta bread (I like wholemeal)
125 ml (4 fl oz/½ cup) tomato pasta
  sauce
1 zucchini (courgette) or 1 large field
  mushroom, sliced
70 g (2½ oz) mozzarella cheese, sliced
1 tablespoon grated parmesan cheese
1 tablespoon fresh oregano leaves
1 tablespoon extra virgin olive oil
sea salt
freshly ground black pepper

Preheat the oven to 240°C (475°F/Gas 8) and put a tray in the oven to heat up. Put
the bread on a piece of baking paper. Spread the bread with tomato sauce and top
with zucchini or mushrooms and then mozzarella. Sprinkle with parmesan and
oregano, drizzle with olive oil and season with salt and pepper. Put the pizza and
paper on the hot tray in the oven and bake for 10 minutes. Makes 1

real fruit jelly

1 litre (35 fl oz/4 cups) cranberry or pink
  grapefruit juice
4 tablespoons powdered gelatine
80 g (2¾ oz/⅓ cup) caster (superfine)
  sugar (optional)

Put about a quarter of the juice in a small bowl and sprinkle the gelatine over the top.
Leave until spongy. Put the rest of the juice in a pan over medium heat and add the
sugar. Stir until dissolved, then add the gelatine and stir until that has dissolved. Pour
into a 23 cm (9 inch) square tray and refrigerate for 3–4 hours until set. Cut into small
squares to serve. Makes 20 squares

fairy bread hearts

1½ tablespoons unsalted butter,
  softened
6 thin slices white bread
2–3 tablespoons hundreds and
  thousands

Butter the bread and sprinkle with hundreds and thousands. Cut two hearts from each
slice with a 6 cm (2½ inch) cutter. Makes 12

Although I like to use wholemeal wherever possible, for
fairy bread it has to be white!

easy-mix chocolate cake with real chocolate frosting

280 g (10 oz/2¼ cups) plain
  (all-purpose) flour
2½ teaspoons baking powder
50 g (1¾ oz) cocoa powder
220 g (8 oz/1 cup) caster (superfine)
  sugar
250 g (9 oz) very soft butter
4 eggs
170 ml (5½ fl oz/⅔ cup) milk

frosting
300 g (10½ oz) dark chocolate, broken
  into pieces
375 ml (13 fl oz/1½ cups) sour cream

to serve
bright sweets (candy) and candles

Preheat the oven to 180°C (350°F/Gas 4). Sift the flour, baking powder, cocoa and sugar into a large bowl and stir together. Add the butter, eggs and milk and mix with electric beaters on low speed for 1–2 minutes until smooth.

Spoon into two greased and lined 20 cm (8 inch) cake tins and bake for 25 minutes or until a skewer inserted into the centre comes out clean. Leave in the tins for 5 minutes before turning out onto wire racks to cool.

Once the cakes are cool, prepare the frosting. Put the chocolate in a stainless steel bowl over a pan of barely simmering water and heat very slowly until the chocolate has just melted, being careful not to let the water boil or touch the bottom of the bowl. Remove from the heat and leave to cool for 15 minutes, before whisking in the sour cream. Use a spatula to spread a third of the frosting over one cake and sandwich with the other. Spread the rest of the frosting over the side and top of the cake. Decorate with sweets and candles if you're celebrating a birthday! Serves 10–12

pure days

I can't bear processed food — whether it's processed in a factory or a restaurant, it makes me miserable. I like my food fresh, clean and pure. I like to be able to taste the ingredients. I love the zing of fresh ginger and lime zest, the sweetness of ocean fish and the spiritual comfort of home-made chicken noodle soup. When I'm run-down or tired, this is the food that makes me feel great. It's energizing, wholesome and very nutritious.

crispy-skinned salmon with anchovy vinaigrette, fennel and green beans

4 x 180 g (6 oz) salmon fillets with skin
2 tablespoons olive oil
sea salt
freshly ground black pepper
2 baby fennel bulbs, finely sliced
250 g (9 oz) baby French beans, topped
  but not tailed, blanched
small handful fresh flat-leaf (Italian)
  parsley

to serve
anchovy vinaigrette, below

Heat a frying pan over medium–high heat for 2 minutes. Brush the salmon with oil and season well with salt and pepper. Cook the salmon, skin side down, for 3 minutes, then turn over and cook for another minute. Remove from the pan and leave to rest for 2 minutes. The salmon should be quite rare and the skin crispy.

Arrange the fennel, beans and parsley on plates. Place the salmon on top and drizzle with anchovy vinaigrette to serve. Serves 4

anchovy vinaigrette

1 small garlic clove
4 anchovies
100 ml (3½ fl oz) extra virgin olive oil
50 ml (1¾ fl oz) red wine vinegar
freshly ground black pepper

In a mortar and pestle, pound the garlic and anchovies to a rough paste. Add the olive oil and red wine vinegar and stir together. Season with pepper (you probably won't need salt).

chicken noodle soup

1.5 litres (52 fl oz/6 cups) chicken stock,
  below
1 parsnip, diced
1 carrot, diced
100 g (3½ oz) lasagne sheets, roughly
  broken into 4 cm (1½ inch) squares
280 g (10 oz/1½ cups) shredded
  chicken (from making the stock, below)
sea salt
white pepper

to serve
chopped fresh flat-leaf (Italian) parsley

Prepare the chicken stock and chicken (see below). Put the chicken stock in a
saucepan over high heat (any extra stock can be frozen). Add the vegetables and
cook for about 10 minutes, until they are just tender. Add the pasta and cook for
another 5 minutes, adding the shredded chicken for the last minute to heat through.
Season with salt and pepper and scatter with parsley to serve. Serves 6–8

chicken stock

1 x 1.5 kg (3 lb 5 oz) chicken
small handful fresh parsley
3 sprigs fresh thyme
½ onion, roughly chopped
2 carrots, roughly chopped
2 celery stalks, roughly chopped
1 teaspoon black peppercorns

Rinse the chicken inside and out and pat dry. Put the chicken in a stockpot with the
rest of the ingredients and 2.5 litres (87 fl oz/10 cups) of cold water. Bring almost to
boiling point, then reduce the heat to low and keep the stock at a steady simmer for
1½ hours, skimming any froth from the surface after the first 5–10 minutes. Lift out the
chicken and strain the stock to get rid of the herbs and vegetables. Let the chicken
cool slightly, then discard the skin and shred the meat.

Some deli stocks are great, but for this soup I always
make my own.

seared tuna with tomato and olive salad

2 x 300 g (10½ oz) tuna steaks
olive oil
sea salt
freshly ground black pepper
3 tablespoons extra virgin olive oil
1 tablespoon red wine vinegar
4 anchovies, roughly chopped
1 garlic clove, finely chopped
1 bird's eye red chilli, finely chopped
300 g (10½ oz) small roma (plum) or
  cherry tomatoes, halved
85 g (3 oz/½ cup) black olives, halved
  and pitted
small handful fresh flat-leaf (Italian)
  parsley
small handful fresh basil leaves

Brush the tuna steaks with a little olive oil and season with salt and pepper. Cook in a large frying pan over high heat for 2–3 minutes on each side.

Mix together the extra virgin olive oil, red wine vinegar, anchovies, garlic and chilli to make a dressing. Slice the tuna and arrange on a plate with the tomato, olives, parsley and basil. Drizzle with the dressing. Serves 4

steamed snapper with lime dressing

2 limes, sliced
2 x 400 g (14 oz) baby snapper
sea salt
2 tablespoons julienned fresh ginger

to serve
small handful coriander (cilantro) leaves
1 large red chilli, seeded and thinly
  sliced
lime dressing, below

Put half the lime slices on a plate in a steamer basket. Lay one of the fish on top, season with salt and top with half the ginger. Place the steamer over a wok or large deep frying pan of boiling water and cook for 8–10 minutes or until the fish is just cooked through. Remove from the heat and repeat with the remaining ingredients to cook the other fish. Sprinkle the fish with coriander and chilli and drizzle the lime dressing over the top to serve. Serves 2

lime dressing

3 tablespoons extra virgin olive oil
3 tablespoons lime juice
1 garlic clove, crushed
½ teaspoon caster (superfine) sugar
sea salt
freshly ground black pepper

Whisk together the olive oil, lime juice, garlic, sugar, salt and pepper.

Fresh is best — buy fish the day you're going to eat it.

ocean trout with red chilli and tomatoes

1 tablespoon olive oil, plus a little
  extra
4 x 200 g (7 oz) ocean trout fillets
2 large red chillies, sliced
5 cm (2 inch) piece of fresh ginger,
  grated
3 garlic cloves, sliced
400 g (14 oz) tomatoes, chopped
2 tablespoons soy sauce
1½ tablespoons sugar

to serve
steamed rice
baby English spinach leaves

Heat the oil in a large frying pan over medium–high heat. Add the trout and cook for
2 minutes on each side or until cooked to your taste. Remove from the pan.

Reduce the heat to medium and add a little extra oil. Add the chilli, ginger and garlic
and cook for 2 minutes until golden. Add the tomatoes, soy sauce and sugar and
cook for 5 minutes, stirring occasionally until thickened.

Serve the trout with steamed rice and baby spinach leaves and the sauce spooned
over the top. Serves 4

To julienne ginger, choose a large piece of fresh ginger and trim to make a rectangle. Slice thinly and then cut the slices into matchsticks.

stir-fried ginger fish with broccolini

1 tablespoon light-flavoured oil (I like canola)
4 tablespoons julienned fresh ginger
350 g (12 oz) firm white fish with skin (I like cod or snapper), cut into bite-sized pieces
8 spring onions (scallions), cut into long lengths
200 g (7 oz) broccolini, sliced diagonally and blanched
2 tablespoons fish sauce
2 teaspoons sugar
1 teaspoon sea salt
2 tablespoons lime juice

to serve
steamed jasmine rice

Heat a wok over medium–high heat. Add the oil and, when hot, stir-fry the ginger for 1 minute. Add the fish and stir-fry for 3 minutes. Add the spring onions, broccolini, fish sauce, sugar and salt and gently stir-fry for another minute. Remove from the heat, add the lime juice and serve with steamed rice. Serves 2

For me, being by the sea is both invigorating and calming.

Another favourite quick salad is a chopped tomato, rocket and cucumber salad. Toss together 4 quartered and chopped Lebanese cucumbers, 4 chopped tomatoes, 150 g (5 oz) shredded rocket (arugula) and 4 finely sliced spring onions (scallions). Stir together 3 tablespoons extra virgin olive oil, 2 tablespoons red wine vinegar and a crushed garlic clove and season with salt and pepper. Pour over the salad and toss well before serving. Serves 4

chicken noodle salad with celery and sesame

1 tablespoon black peppercorns
2 spring onions (scallions), roughly chopped
2 tablespoons sea salt
2 chicken breasts
375 g (13 oz) fresh egg noodles
2 teaspoons sesame oil
3 tablespoons soy sauce
2 tablespoons caster (superfine) sugar
3 tablespoons lime juice
6 spring onions (scallions), julienned
200 g (7 oz) snow peas (mangetout), blanched and cut in half diagonally
2 celery stalks, sliced diagonally
2 Lebanese cucumbers, finely sliced diagonally
2 teaspoons sesame seeds

Put the peppercorns, chopped spring onions and salt in a large saucepan, fill with cold water and bring to the boil over high heat. Add the chicken breasts and stir. Turn off the heat, cover with a tight-fitting lid and leave for 1 hour. Shred the chicken.

Cook the noodles according to the packet instructions. Drain, refresh under cold water and then drain again. Mix together the sesame oil, soy sauce, sugar and lime juice to make a dressing. Toss half the dressing through the noodles and arrange on a plate. Top with the chicken, julienned spring onions, snow peas, celery and cucumber. Drizzle with the remaining dressing and sprinkle with sesame seeds. Serves 4

beetroot salad

18 baby beetroot (beets)
150 g (5½ oz) rocket (arugula)
150 g (5½ oz) sugar snap peas,
  blanched, refreshed and trimmed
2 blood oranges, peeled and sliced
3 tablespoons extra virgin olive oil
1½ tablespoons white wine vinegar
1 teaspoon chopped fresh oregano
sea salt
freshly ground black pepper

Trim the beetroot, reserving some of the nicest leaves. Cook the beetroot in boiling salted water for 30–40 minutes or until tender. Rinse under running water and peel away the skin.

Arrange the beetroot leaves, beetroot, rocket, sugar snaps and blood oranges on a platter. Mix together the olive oil, white wine vinegar, oregano, salt and pepper and drizzle over the salad. Serves 4

To prepare the beetroot, cut the stems, leaving 2–3 cm (about 1 inch) attached to the bulb. Wash well but don't cut off the root or the colour will bleed out during the cooking. Once you've cooked the beetroot, rub off the skins under running water (you could wear rubber gloves to avoid getting pink hands).

carrot, feta and mint salad

1 kg (2 lb 4 oz) carrots, peeled, halved
  and sliced
2 garlic cloves, crushed
3 tablespoons lemon juice
3 tablespoons extra virgin olive oil
2 teaspoons ground cumin
2 teaspoons paprika
1 teaspoon sea salt
freshly ground black pepper
150 g (5½ oz) feta cheese
small handful fresh mint leaves
45 g (1¾ oz/⅓ cup) black olives, sliced

Cook the carrots in boiling salted water for 1 minute. Drain and refresh in iced water. Stir together the garlic, lemon juice, olive oil, cumin, paprika, salt and pepper. Arrange the carrots on a serving platter. Top with the crumbled feta, mint and olives and drizzle the dressing over the top. Serves 4

I love these salads with a simple piece of grilled meat or fish.

Look for tuna that has firm, dark, meaty flesh (almost the colour of spring lamb is a good guide). Try to avoid pieces that have the bloodline running through them. But really, the best advice for buying fish is to find a good fish shop.

linguine with yellow-fin tuna, capers and olives

3 tablespoons extra virgin olive oil
2 tablespoons salted capers, rinsed
500 g (1 lb 2 oz) linguine
400 g (14 oz) yellow-fin tuna, thinly
  sliced
1 large red chilli, finely sliced
12 large green olives, finely sliced
100 g (3½ oz) wild rocket (arugula)
2 tablespoons lemon juice
sea salt
freshly ground black pepper

Heat 1 tablespoon of the olive oil in a frying pan over high heat, add the capers and cook for 1 minute or until golden.

Cook the pasta in a large saucepan of boiling salted water until *al dente*. Drain and place in a bowl with the capers, tuna, chilli, olives, rocket, lemon juice, salt, pepper and remaining olive oil. Toss gently to combine. Serves 4

glazed salmon with brown rice

2 tablespoons julienned fresh ginger
2 garlic cloves, sliced
3 tablespoons oyster sauce
3 tablespoons sweet chilli sauce (bought
 or see page 190)
1 tablespoon soy sauce
700 g (1 lb 9 oz) salmon fillet
200 g (7 oz) bok choy (pak choy)
1 tablespoon mirin
1 tablespoon soy sauce

to serve
steamed brown rice

Stir together the ginger, garlic, oyster sauce, sweet chilli sauce and soy sauce in a
large bowl. Cut the salmon fillet into large chunks, add to the bowl and leave to
marinate in the fridge for at least 15 minutes and up to 1 hour.

Preheat the grill (broiler). Arrange the salmon chunks in a single layer on a large
baking tray and cook under the hot grill for 7 minutes (the fish should still be pink in
the centre).

Meanwhile, halve the bok choy and steam or blanch for 1 minute, or until tender but
still bright green and crisp. Spoon the brown rice into serving bowls, top with the
salmon and pan juices and serve with bok choy. Mix together the mirin and soy sauce
and drizzle over the bok choy. Serves 4

I don't use brown rice to be virtuous — I just love
the nutty flavour.

baking days

As much as fashions change in food, baking is a true constant. There are not many recipes my mother made thirty years ago that have made it into the twenty-first century (her tinned pears with crème de menthe jelly springs to mind) but her baked cheesecake is still wonderfully relevant today. Everyone who knows me knows how I love teatime with scones and teacakes, fancy sandwiches and a great smell wafting from the oven. In this hectic world I think it's something we should all enjoy as often as we can.

cucumber and chive sandwiches

12 slices white bread
250 g (9 oz/1 cup) cream cheese,
  softened
3 Lebanese cucumbers, thinly sliced
2 tablespoons snipped chives
20 g (¾ oz) salad leaves
sea salt
freshly ground black pepper

Spread half the bread with the cream cheese and arrange the cucumber slices over
the cream cheese. Top with the chives and salad leaves and season with salt and
pepper. Sandwich with the remaining slices of bread, trim the crusts and cut in half
to serve. Makes 12

For neat little sandwiches, snip chives and
salad leaves with kitchen scissors.

chicken finger sandwiches

1 tablespoon black peppercorns
2 spring onions (scallions), roughly
  chopped
2 tablespoons sea salt
2 chicken breasts
12 slices wholemeal (whole-wheat)
  bread
250 ml (9 fl oz/1 cup) whole-egg
  mayonnaise
2 celery stalks, thinly sliced, with leaves
small handful chopped fresh flat-leaf
  (Italian) parsley
sea salt
freshly ground black pepper

Put the peppercorns, chopped spring onions and salt in a large saucepan, fill with
cold water and bring to the boil over high heat. Add the chicken breasts and stir. Turn
off the heat, cover with a tight-fitting lid and leave for 1 hour. Slice the chicken.

Spread half the bread with the mayonnaise and top with the chicken, celery and
leaves, parsley and salt and pepper. Sandwich with the remaining slices of bread, trim
the crusts and cut in half to serve. Makes 12

cinnamon tea cake

sultana scones

1 tablespoon icing (confectioners') sugar
310 g (11 oz/2½ cups) plain
  (all-purpose) flour
1½ tablespoons baking powder
pinch of salt
60 g (2¼ oz/½ cup) sultanas (golden
  raisins)
1 teaspoon orange zest
250 ml (9 fl oz/1 cup) milk
30 g (1 oz) unsalted butter, melted

to serve
butter and raspberry jam

Preheat the oven to 220°C (425°F/Gas 7). Sift the icing sugar, flour, baking powder and salt into a bowl. Add the sultanas and orange zest and stir to combine. Add the milk and butter and stir with a knife to combine. Knead quickly and lightly until smooth and then press out on a floured surface to about 3 cm (1¼ inches) thick.

Use a cutter or glass to cut 5 cm (2 inch) rounds. Place close together on a greased baking tray. Gather the scraps together, knead again and cut out more rounds. Cook for about 10 minutes until puffed and golden. Serve with butter and jam. Makes 12

natalie's cinnamon tea cake

60 g (2¼ oz) unsalted butter
145 g (5 oz/⅔ cup) caster (superfine)
  sugar
1 egg
1 teaspoon natural vanilla extract
155 g (5½ oz/1¼ cups) plain
  (all-purpose) flour
1 teaspoon baking powder
80 ml (2½ fl oz/⅓ cup) milk

topping
3 teaspoons caster (superfine) sugar
¾ teaspoon ground cinnamon
10 g (¼ oz) unsalted butter

Preheat the oven to 180°C (350°F/Gas 4). Beat the butter and sugar with electric beaters or a wooden spoon until pale and creamy. Add the egg and vanilla and stir together. Sift in the flour and baking powder, add the milk and mix until combined.

Pour into a greased and lined 20 cm (8 inch) cake tin and bake for 20 minutes, or until a skewer inserted into the centre comes out clean. Leave in the tin for 2 minutes before turning out onto a plate.

To make the topping, mix together the sugar and cinnamon. Dot the warm cake with butter and brush to melt. Sprinkle with the cinnamon sugar and serve warm. Serves 8

peach, almond and yoghurt cake

220 g (7¾ oz) unsalted butter, softened
250 g (9 oz) caster (superfine) sugar
1 teaspoon natural vanilla extract
3 eggs
310 g (11 oz/2½ cups) self-raising flour,
  sifted
50 ml (1¾ fl oz) milk
250 g (9 oz/1 cup) plain yoghurt
1 tablespoon amaretto (optional)
450 g (1 lb) small peaches, chopped
50 g (1¾ oz) flaked almonds

to serve
125 ml (4 fl oz/½ cup) plain yoghurt
125 ml (4 fl oz/½ cup) cream

Look for highly coloured, fragrant and
firm peaches with just a little bit of 'give'.
Freestone peaches are easier to use for
cooking: the peach flesh falls away easily
from the stone (as opposed to the aptly
named clingstone peaches).

Preheat the oven to 170ºC (325ºF/Gas 3). Grease and line the base of a 23 cm
(9 inch) springform tin. Beat the butter and sugar with electric beaters until light and
fluffy. Add the vanilla, then add the eggs one at a time, beating well after each
addition. Add half the flour, the milk and half the yoghurt and mix at low speed for
1 minute. Add the remaining flour and yoghurt with the amaretto and mix until
combined. Gently fold through the peaches.

Pour the mixture into the tin and sprinkle with the almonds. Bake for 1½ hours or until
a skewer inserted into the centre comes out clean. If it is browning too quickly, cover
the top of the cake with foil for the last 20 minutes. Leave to cool. Whip together the
yoghurt and cream until thick and serve with the cake. Serves 10–12

I love the combination of fruit and cake — the tang with
the sweet.

mini caramel tarts

250 g (9 oz/2 cups) plain (all-purpose) flour
115 g (4 oz/½ cup) caster (superfine) sugar
115 g (4 oz) butter
1 egg

filling
450 g (1 lb) caster (superfine) sugar
185 ml (6 fl oz/¾ cup) cream
40 g (1½ oz) unsalted butter
chocolate buttons

Mix the flour, sugar and butter in a food processor until fine crumbs form. Add the egg and pulse until just combined. Turn out and knead lightly. Wrap in plastic and chill for 20 minutes. Roll out the dough to 4 mm (¼ inch) thick and cut out 6.5 cm (2½ inch) rounds. Place in two 12-hole patty tins and put in the freezer for 15–20 minutes. Preheat the oven to 200°C (400°F/Gas 6). Bake for 15 minutes, until just golden.

To make the filling, put the sugar in a pan with 250 ml (9 fl oz/1 cup) of water and boil over high heat for 15 minutes until deep golden. Remove from the heat, stir in the cream carefully and the butter. Pour over the biscuit bases and chill for 2 hours. Decorate with chocolate buttons and keep in the fridge until ready to serve. Makes 24

friands

135 g (4¾ oz/1⅓ cups) ground almonds
220 g (7¾ oz/1¾ cups) icing
  (confectioners') sugar, sifted, plus a
  little extra for dusting
85 g (3 oz/⅔ cup) plain (all-purpose)
  flour, sifted
8 egg whites
150 g (5½ oz) unsalted butter, melted
210 g (7½ oz/1½ cups) cherries or
  115 g (4 oz/ 1 cup) raspberries or
  3 nectarines, chopped

Preheat the oven to 180°C (350°F/Gas 4). Grease and flour a non-stick 12-hole friand tin. Mix together the ground almonds, icing sugar and flour. Stir in the egg whites until just combined. Stir in the melted butter.

Pour the batter into the tins. Pit the cherries and cut in half. Arrange a few cherry halves or raspberries or nectarine pieces on top of each friand.

Bake for 25–30 minutes or until pale and golden. The friands should spring back when touched. Remove from the oven and leave in the tin for 5 minutes before turning out onto a wire rack to cool. Dust with icing sugar and store in an airtight container. Makes 12

Friands can be made with just about any fruit (I also like mango and lime zest) or even tiny chunks of chocolate.

All the rolling, flouring, cutting and general mess-making of baking is very therapeutic.

I prefer to chop up a block of good-quality chocolate than buy commercial choc chips.

double chocolate chip cookies

250 g (9 oz) unsalted butter, softened
350 g (12 oz) soft brown sugar
1 teaspoon natural vanilla extract
2 eggs, lightly beaten
310 g (11 oz/2½ cups) plain
  (all-purpose) flour
60 g (2¼ oz/½ cup) cocoa powder
2 teaspoons baking powder
2 teaspoons sea salt
350 g (12 oz) dark chocolate, chopped

Preheat the oven to 180°C (350°F/Gas 4). Beat together the butter and sugar until light and creamy. Add the vanilla and eggs and stir together well. Sift in the flour, cocoa powder, baking powder and salt and mix until just combined. Fold in the chocolate. Place large spoonfuls of the mixture on a greased and paper-lined baking tray, leaving room for spreading. Cook in batches for 15–20 minutes, until the bases are cooked. Cool on the trays. Makes about 30

Baking is an easy way to introduce kids to cooking.

mum's baked lime cheesecake

100 g (3½ oz/1 cup) crushed wholemeal
  biscuits (graham crackers)
55 g (2 oz/½ cup) ground almonds
50 g (1¾ oz) unsalted butter, melted
  and cooled
800 g (1 lb 12 oz) light cream cheese
185 g (6½ oz/¾ cup) light sour cream
175 g (6 oz/¾ cup) caster (superfine)
  sugar
4 eggs, plus 2 egg whites
1 tablespoon lime zest
1½ tablespoons lime juice

to serve
3–4 mangoes

Preheat the oven to 150°C (300°F/Gas 2). Grease a 24 cm (9½ inch) springform tin
and line the base. To make the base, mix together the biscuits, almonds and
melted butter and press into the base of the tin, patting down well. Refrigerate for
15 minutes.

To make the filling, beat the cream cheese, sour cream and sugar until light and fluffy.
Add the eggs, two at a time, beating well after each addition. Add the lime zest and
juice and mix well. Beat the egg whites in a separate bowl until stiff peaks form, then
fold into the cream cheese mixture. Pour over the base.

Bake for 1 hour 10 minutes on a low rack. (The cheesecake will not be completely set
in the centre.) Turn off the oven and leave the cheesecake inside to cool with the door
open for 30 minutes. Remove from the oven and leave at room temperature for
another 2–3 hours, until completely cooled. Refrigerate overnight.

To remove the cheesecake from the tin, carefully run a hot knife around the outside,
then slide off the base of the tin.

Cut the mangoes in half on either side of the stone. Cut the flesh in a cross-cross
pattern on each cheek and then push inside out. Serve with the lime cheesecake.
Serves 10–12

almond biscuits

310 g (11 oz/2 cups) blanched almonds
3 egg whites
330 g (11¾ oz/1½ cups) caster
  (superfine) sugar
4½ tablespoons plain (all-purpose) flour
sugar, for sprinkling

Preheat the oven to 180°C (350°F/Gas 4). Finely grind the almonds in a food processor. Beat the egg whites until stiff peaks form. Fold the ground almonds into the egg whites and mix in the caster sugar and flour.

Roll tablespoons of the dough into balls and place on a greased and paper-lined baking tray. Sprinkle with sugar and bake for 15 minutes or until golden. Makes 30

coconut macaroons

2 egg whites
115 g (4 oz/½ cup) caster (superfine)
  sugar
150 g (5½ oz/2 cups) shredded coconut
100 g (3½ oz/¾ cup) roughly chopped
  macadamia nuts
1 teaspoon lime zest

Preheat the oven to 160°C (315°F/Gas 2–3). Mix together the egg whites, caster sugar, coconut, nuts and lime zest in a bowl (you may need to use your hands).

Shape tablespoons of the mixture into mounds on paper-lined baking trays. Bake for 10–15 minutes or until light golden brown. Cool on the trays. Makes 20

I sometimes serve coconut macaroons as a dessert with a scoop of coconut ice cream.

apricot bars

155 g (5½ oz/1¼ cups) plain
  (all-purpose) flour
95 g (3½ oz/½ cup) soft brown sugar
115 g (4 oz/½ cup) caster (superfine)
  sugar
2 pinches of salt
1 teaspoon baking powder
175 g (6 oz) unsalted butter,
  chilled and diced

130 g (4½ oz/1 cup) rolled oats
90 g (3¼ oz/1 cup) desiccated coconut
450 g (1 lb/2½ cups) chopped dried
  apricots
100 g (3½ oz/⅓ cup) apricot jam
40 g (1½ oz) unsalted butter, melted

Preheat the oven to 180°C (350°F/Gas 4). Mix the flour, sugars, salt, baking powder
and butter in a food processor until a dough forms. (Or, rub the ingredients together
with your fingertips.) Mix in the oats and coconut. Reserve a cupful of dough and
press the remainder evenly into a lightly greased and lined 20 x 30 cm (8 x 12 inch)
baking tin. Bake for 15 minutes until golden.

Put the apricots and 125 ml (4 fl oz/½ cup) of water in a small pan over low heat and
cook, stirring occasionally, until the liquid has been absorbed. Cool slightly, then
spoon over the dough base. Dot the jam over the apricots and crumble the reserved
dough over the top. Spoon on the melted butter and bake for 30–35 minutes until
lightly golden. Leave to cool completely in the tray. Slice into squares and store in an
airtight container. Makes 24

special days

I think entertaining should be about the whole meal — not just the food, but the drinks, music, decorations and mood. I love choosing a theme and getting carried away with the details. Having said that, I'm not hugely in favour of formal dinners and I rarely serve a three-course sit-down meal. If you come around to our house you'll find all the dishes — nibbles, starters, mains and sides — put on the table at the same time. And the food will still be simple (it is just not in my nature to overwork things), just put together in a different way. The one thing I do have rules for, though, is flavours. In these times when we might eat Italian, sushi and Mexican all in the course of one day, I like the flavours of each menu to be complementary and consistent.

summer salsa dinner guacamole with toasted tortilla chips, tequila mojito, marinated king prawns, corn rice salad

guacamole with toasted tortilla chips

1 small white onion, finely diced
1 teaspoon sea salt
1 fresh green chilli, seeded
 and finely chopped
juice of 2 limes
2 ripe avocados, diced
2 small tomatoes, seeded and diced
handful fresh coriander (cilantro) leaves
240 g (8½ oz) packet of flour tortillas

Put the onion, salt and chilli in a mortar and pestle and pound together lightly. Add the lime juice, avocado, tomato and coriander and stir through.

Cut the tortillas into triangles and toast under the grill (broiler) for 1 minute on each side until lightly browned and crisp. Serve with the guacamole. Serves 4

tequila mojito

large handful fresh mint leaves
110 g (3¾ oz/½ cup) sugar
4 tablespoons lime juice
170 ml (5½ fl oz/⅔ cup) white tequila
crushed ice
325 ml (11 fl oz) chilled sparkling water

Put the mint leaves and sugar in a mixing glass and crush together with a pestle or the end of a rolling pin. Stir in the lime juice and tequila.

Fill four glasses with crushed ice and pour the tequila mixture over the top. Fill up with sparkling water. Serves 4

Finish off with slices of fresh papaya. Cut the fruit in half, remove the seeds and slice into neat wedges. Squeeze a lime over the top.

marinated king prawns

12 large raw prawns (shrimp)
4 garlic cloves, crushed
1 small red chilli, seeded and chopped
4 tablespoons extra virgin olive oil
sea salt

to serve
lime wedges

Soak 12 bamboo skewers in water for a few hours beforehand to prevent them scorching on the barbecue.

Peel and devein the prawns, leaving the tails intact. Mix together the garlic, chilli and oil and pour over the prawns. Leave for 30 minutes to marinate.

Preheat a barbecue or chargrill pan. Thread the prawns onto skewers, sprinkle with salt and cook for 2–3 minutes on each side until lightly charred. Serve with lime wedges. Serves 4

corn rice salad

200 g (7 oz/1 cup) short-grain rice
400 g (14 oz/2 cups) fresh corn kernels
2 tablespoons extra virgin olive oil
3 tablespoons lime juice
sea salt
freshly ground black pepper
small handful fresh coriander (cilantro)
  leaves
4 spring onions (scallions), chopped

Cook the rice in boiling salted water for 10 minutes or until tender. Add the corn kernels for the last 30 seconds, then drain and refresh under cold water.

Combine the oil and lime juice in a serving bowl and season with salt and pepper. Tip the rice mixture into the dressing and toss to coat. Just before serving, toss through the coriander leaves and spring onions. Serves 4

farmhouse lunch thyme-roasted almonds, gnocchi with fresh tomato sauce, simple roast chicken, green salad with shallot vinaigrette, cherry clafoutis

thyme-roasted almonds

thyme-roasted almonds

250 g (9 oz/1⅔ cups) raw almonds
1 tablespoon extra virgin olive oil
2 teaspoons chopped fresh thyme
2 teaspoons sea salt

Preheat the oven to 200°C (400°F/Gas 6). Put all the ingredients in a bowl and toss together. Transfer to a paper-lined baking tray and bake for 5–7 minutes. Leave to cool before serving with drinks. Serves 4–6

gnocchi with fresh tomato sauce

500 g (1 lb 2 oz) ripe tomatoes or
  400 g (14 oz) tinned tomatoes
2 tablespoons extra virgin olive oil, plus
  extra for the gnocchi
3 garlic cloves, thinly sliced
a pinch of sugar
1 teaspoon sea salt
500 g (1 lb 2 oz) good-quality potato
  gnocchi

to serve
fresh basil leaves

Score a cross in the base of each tomato, put in a bowl and pour boiling water over the top. Soak for 30 seconds, then drain and refresh under cold water. Peel away the skin from the cross and roughly chop the tomato flesh.

Heat the oil in a heavy-based frying pan over medium heat. Add the garlic and cook for 1 minute until golden. Add the tomatoes, sugar and sea salt and cook over medium–low heat, stirring occasionally, for 20 minutes until thickened.

Meanwhile, bring a large saucepan of salted water to the boil, add the gnocchi and cook until they rise to the surface. Drain and toss with a little extra oil to prevent them sticking together. Top with the tomato sauce and garnish with fresh basil leaves to serve. Serves 4

simple roast chicken

1 x 1.6 kg (3 lb 8 oz) chicken
sea salt
freshly ground black pepper
handful fresh herbs (such as oregano,
  thyme or tarragon)
2 garlic cloves, bruised
2 lemons, halved

to serve
handful fresh herbs (whichever you used
  for the roasting)

Preheat the oven to 220°C (425°F/Gas 7). Rinse the chicken and pat dry. Season
well with salt and pepper. Put the herbs, garlic and two lemon halves in the chicken
cavity and tie the legs together with kitchen string. Put the chicken in a roasting tin
with the other lemon halves and roast for 20 minutes.

Reduce the oven temperature to 200°C (400°F/Gas 6) and cook for 50 minutes, or
until the juices run clear when you prick the thickest part of the thigh. Leave to rest
for 10 minutes before carving. Serve the chicken with its pan juices, the roast lemon
halves and some fresh herbs. Serves 4

green salad with shallot vinaigrette

1 French shallot, finely diced
1 tablespoon red wine vinegar
sea salt
freshly ground black pepper
3 tablespoons extra virgin olive oil
200 g (7 oz) salad leaves

Put the shallot and vinegar in a small bowl and season with salt and pepper. Whisk in
the olive oil, pour over the salad leaves and toss to combine. Serves 4

For relaxed dining I put everything on the table together
and serve the gnocchi with the chicken.

cherry clafoutis

butter, for greasing
250 g (9 oz) cherries, pitted
4 tablespoons plain (all-purpose) flour, sifted
110 g (3¾ oz/½ cup) caster (superfine) sugar
125 ml (4 fl oz/½ cup) milk
185 ml (6 fl oz/¾ cup) cream
1 teaspoon natural vanilla extract
4 eggs

to serve
cream or crème fraîche

Preheat the oven to 180°C (350°F/Gas 4). Grease a 1.5 litre (52 fl oz/6 cup) flan dish with butter and dust with a little caster sugar, then arrange the cherries in the dish. Mix the flour and sugar in a bowl, add the milk, cream and vanilla and whisk together. Add the eggs and whisk until smooth. Pour over the cherries and bake for 30–35 minutes or until puffed and golden. Serve warm with cream or crème fraîche. Serves 8–10

If you were living in France, you probably wouldn't pit the cherries, but I find it less dangerous for everyone's teeth if you do. You can buy a special cherry pitter that makes it an easy job.

People are surprised that what I love to do in my time off is more cooking.

pool **party** glazed ham, fresh mango chutney, spicy 'slaw, dill potato salad, green bean salad, fresh passionfruit trifle

glazed ham

6 kg (13 lb) leg ham
20–25 whole cloves
170 ml (5½ fl oz/⅔ cup) honey
2 tablespoons wholegrain mustard
3 tablespoons dry sherry or rum
2 teaspoons soy sauce
3 tablespoons soft brown sugar

Preheat the oven to 180°C (350°F/Gas 4).

Use a small sharp knife to cut through the rind around the shank of the ham. Carefully lift the rind from the fat in one piece, running your fingers through where they are joined to ease lifting.

Score the white fat in a diamond pattern and press a clove into the centre of each diamond. Place the ham on a rack over a paper-lined roasting tin and bake for 10 minutes.

To make the glaze, put the honey, mustard, sherry, soy sauce and sugar in a saucepan over low heat, stirring to dissolve the sugar, and simmer for 10 minutes or until thickened. Brush over the ham, making sure that all the exposed fat is covered. Bake the ham for 20–30 minutes, basting every 10 minutes, until it is golden. Remove from the oven and transfer the ham to a platter. Serve with fresh mango chutney. Serves 8–10

fresh mango chutney

½ small red onion, finely diced
1 red chilli, seeded and finely chopped
3 ripe mangoes, diced
2 tablespoons lime juice
1 teaspoon caster (superfine) sugar
sea salt

Gently stir together all the ingredients in a bowl. Leave to rest for at least 30 minutes to let the flavours combine.

spicy 'slaw

125 ml (4 fl oz/½ cup) extra virgin olive oil
4 tablespoons lime juice
sea salt
freshly ground black pepper
½ cabbage, finely shredded
1 red onion, finely sliced
small handful fresh coriander (cilantro)
2 large red chillies, finely sliced

Whisk together the oil, lime juice, salt and pepper to make a dressing. Mix together
the cabbage and red onion, add the dressing and stir gently. Cover and refrigerate
until ready to serve. Add the coriander leaves and chilli. Serves 4–6

dill potato salad

1 kg (2 lb 4 oz) kipfler (fingerling)
  potatoes, unpeeled
6 spring onions (scallions), chopped
small handful roughly chopped fresh flat-
  leaf (Italian) parsley
small handful finely chopped fresh dill

1 tablespoon caster (superfine) sugar
1 tablespoon dijon mustard
sea salt
freshly ground black pepper
2 tablespoons white wine vinegar
4 tablespoons extra virgin olive oil

Cook the potatoes in boiling salted water until soft. Drain and slice. Gently mix with
the spring onions, parsley and dill. Whisk together the sugar, mustard, salt, pepper
and vinegar and then add the oil in a thin stream, whisking until slightly thickened.
Add the potatoes and leave to cool before serving. Serves 4–6

green bean salad

3 tablespoons extra virgin olive oil
1 tablespoon white wine vinegar
sea salt
freshly ground black pepper
300 g (10½ oz) green beans, blanched
250 g (9 oz) yellow teardrop tomatoes,
  halved
3 spring onions (scallions), sliced
small handful fresh flat-leaf (Italian)
  parsley leaves

Whisk together the oil, vinegar, salt and pepper to make a dressing. Mix the beans,
tomatoes, spring onions and parsley and toss with the dressing. Serves 4–6

To make great ice cream cones at home, fold chopped dark chocolate through a tub of softened vanilla ice cream. Refreeze to firm the ice cream and then scoop into the best waffle cones you can buy.

fresh passionfruit trifle

passionfruit syrup
250 ml (9 fl oz/1 cup) passionfruit pulp
  (from about 12 passionfruit)
115 g (4 oz/½ cup) caster (superfine)
  sugar

300 ml (10½ fl oz) cream
2 tablespoons dessert wine
2 tablespoons icing (confectioners')
  sugar
1 teaspoon natural vanilla extract
600 g (1 lb 5 oz) sponge cake, cut into
  cubes
250 ml (9 fl oz/1 cup) dessert wine,
  extra

To make the passionfruit syrup, put the passionfruit pulp, sugar and 125 ml (4 fl oz/ ½ cup) of water in a saucepan over medium heat. Stir to dissolve the sugar and then boil for 10 minutes until the syrup has a jammy consistency. Leave to cool.

Whisk together the cream, dessert wine, icing sugar and vanilla until soft peaks form.

Place half the sponge into six serving dishes, drizzle with half the extra dessert wine, top with half the cream and half the passionfruit syrup. Repeat the layers once more. Serves 6

ridiculously easy dinner party
breaded chicken with mustard,
tomato salad with preserved lemon,
figs and raspberries with fresh ricotta,
almond bread

breaded chicken with mustard

8 chicken thighs on the bone, with skin
3 tablespoons dijon mustard
2 eggs, lightly beaten
40 g (1½ oz/½ cup) fresh breadcrumbs
1 tablespoon chopped fresh flat-leaf
  (Italian) parsley
pinch of dried red chilli flakes
sea salt
freshly ground black pepper
25 g (1 oz) butter

to serve
boiled new potatoes

If you ever need a super-quick starter, trim
some asparagus spears and then simmer in
salted water for a couple of minutes to just
soften. Serve them on a platter, drizzled with
extra virgin olive oil and sprinkled with sea
salt and parmesan shavings.

Preheat the oven to 180°C (350°F/Gas 4). Spread the chicken pieces with mustard,
then dip in the beaten egg and put in a lightly oiled baking dish.

Mix together the breadcrumbs, parsley, chilli, salt and pepper in a bowl. Sprinkle
evenly over the chicken. Dot with butter and bake for 35 minutes, until the chicken
is golden brown. Serve with boiled new potatoes. Serves 4

tomato salad with preserved lemon

4 tomatoes, cut into wedges
2 salad onion bulbs, thinly sliced into
  rings
small handful fresh flat-leaf (Italian)
  parsley
small handful watercress, trimmed
2 tablespoons olive oil
1 tablespoon lemon juice
1 tablespoon finely chopped preserved
  lemon, pith and flesh removed

Put all the ingredients in a salad bowl and toss together gently. Serves 4

You can buy supermarket packets of mini ice creams these days that are perfect for serving with coffee at the end of a casual dinner. For elegance, serve them (sticks upwards) in a bowl in the centre of the table (you could chill the bowl in the freezer beforehand).

figs and raspberries with fresh ricotta

500 g (1 lb 2 oz) piece fresh ricotta
120 g (4¼ oz) perfect raspberries
4 figs, sliced
runny honey

to serve

almond bread, below or bought

Cut the ricotta into four wedges and arrange on serving plates. Top with the raspberries and figs and drizzle with honey. Serve with almond bread or biscuits.
Serves 4

almond bread

250 g (9 oz) caster (superfine) sugar
185 g (6½ oz/1½ cups) plain
 (all-purpose) flour
185 g (6½ oz/1½ cups) self-raising flour
200 g (7 oz/1⅓ cups) blanched almonds
5 egg whites

Preheat the oven to 150ºC (300ºF/Gas 2). Mix together the sugar, flours and almonds in a large bowl. Add the egg whites and stir to combine. Flour your hands and bring together to form a soft sticky dough. Press into a paper-lined, greased and floured 27 x 7 x 7 cm (11 x 3 x 3 inch) tin and bake for 1 hour 20 minutes or until golden. Set aside to cool completely.

Remove the bread from the tin and slice as thinly as you can. Arrange the slices on a paper-lined baking tray and return to the oven in batches for 5 minutes until light golden. Cool completely before serving. Store in an airtight container.
Makes 45 pieces

celebration drinks scallops with garlic butter, crab and cucumber salad, pumpernickel with cheat's gravlax, baked saffron arancini, sorbet with vodka, rum berry cooler

To make fresh coconut shavings, pierce a hole through the soft eye of the coconut and drain out the juice. Put the coconut in a 200°C (400°F/Gas 6) oven for 20 minutes. Hold the warm coconut in a towel and crack it with a heavy implement, like the back of a cleaver. Use a blunt knife to remove the flesh from the shell while it's still warm and then make shavings with a vegetable peeler.

scallops with garlic butter

12 scallops on the shell
60 g (2 oz) butter, softened
1 garlic clove, crushed
zest of 1 lime
1 teaspoon fresh thyme leaves
sea salt

Preheat the grill (broiler). Put the scallops on a tray. Mix together the butter and garlic and spoon on top of the scallops. Sprinkle with lime zest and thyme and cook under the hot grill for 2 minutes, or until just cooked. Season with sea salt and serve.
Makes 12

crab and cucumber salad

150 g (5½ oz) vermicelli noodles
300 g (10½ oz) crab meat
1 small cucumber, thinly sliced
1 long red chilli, finely sliced
2 tablespoons fresh mint leaves
200 g (7 oz) snow peas (mangetout),
  blanched and sliced
shavings of fresh coconut

coconut and lime dressing
80 ml (2½ fl oz/⅓ cup) coconut cream
2 tablespoons lime juice
1 tablespoon caster (superfine) sugar
1 tablespoon fish sauce

Pour boiling water over the noodles and leave for 5 minutes to soften. Drain and refresh under cold water, then drain and set aside.

To make the dressing, stir together the coconut cream, lime juice, caster sugar and fish sauce until the sugar has dissolved.

Put the noodles in a bowl with the crab meat, cucumber, chilli, mint leaves and snow peas. Pour the dressing over the top and toss gently. Top with the coconut shavings.
Serves 6

pumpernickel with cheat's gravlax

6 slices pumpernickel
2 tablespoons chopped fresh dill
2 tablespoons chopped fresh chervil
2 tablespoons snipped chives
½ teaspoon lemon zest
250 g (9 oz) piece salmon fillet, kept
  cold in the fridge, skin removed
2 tablespoons lemon juice
2 tablespoons extra virgin olive oil

Cut each slice of pumpernickel into four squares. Mix together the dill, chervil, chives and lemon zest. Press one side of the salmon into the herb mix to coat it. Put the salmon, herb side up, on a chopping board and use a very sharp knife to slice it as thinly as you can. Arrange on top of the pumpernickel and drizzle with the combined lemon juice and oil just before serving. Makes 24 squares

baked saffron arancini

3 tablespoons olive oil
25 g (1 oz) butter
1 white onion, finely chopped
sea salt
250 g (9 oz) arborio rice
½ teaspoon saffron threads
375 ml (13 fl oz/1½ cups) chicken stock
50 g (1¾ oz/½ cup grated parmesan
  cheese
freshly ground black pepper
3 tablespoons chopped fresh flat-leaf
  (Italian) parsley
60 g (2 oz) mozzarella, diced

60 g (2¼ oz/½ cup) plain (all-purpose)
  flour
3 eggs, lightly beaten
100 g (3½ oz/1 cup) dry breadcrumbs

Heat a large heavy-based saucepan and add 1 tablespoon olive oil, half the butter, the onion and salt. Cook over low heat, stirring occasionally, until the onion is softened but not browned. Add the rice and saffron and stir for a few minutes to coat. Increase the heat to high, add the chicken stock and 250 ml (9 fl oz/1 cup) of water and bring to the boil. Cover the pan and cook for 15 minutes, stirring occasionally.

Remove from the heat and stir in the remaining butter with the parmesan and black pepper. Transfer to a large bowl and refrigerate for 15 minutes. Stir in the parsley. Wet your hands (so that the rice doesn't stick) and roll the mixture into balls, using about 1 tablespoon for each. Push a cube of mozzarella into the centre of each ball.

Preheat the oven to 200°C (400°F/Gas 6). Put the flour, egg and breadcrumbs in separate bowls. Dip each ball in the flour, then the egg and then roll in the breadcrumbs. Drizzle the oil over a baking tray. Put the balls on the tray, roll in the remaining olive oil and bake for 25 minutes until golden. Makes 30

sorbet with vodka

1 litre (35 fl oz/4 cups) good-quality
  sorbet (passionfruit, mango
  or strawberry)
500 ml (17 fl oz/2 cups) vodka

Scoop the sorbet into small glasses or bowls. Drizzle 1–2 tablespoons of vodka over the top of each serving. Serve immediately with spoons. Makes 12

rum berry cooler

1 cup ice cubes
2 tablespoons white rum
2 tablespoons lime juice
50 g (1¾ oz/½ cup) raspberries
2 teaspoons sugar
soda water
2 slices lime

to serve
ice cubes

Put the ice, rum, lime juice, raspberries and sugar in a cocktail shaker. Shake and strain into two glasses half-filled with ice. Top with a dash of soda and a slice of lime. Serves 2

rum berry cooler

Seal the edges of the won ton wrappers to make triangles and then fold down the points of each triangle so that the won tons are shaped like tortellini.

chinese banquet prawn won tons with sweet chilli dipping sauce, sticky spare ribs, snow pea salad with sesame seeds, rice salad with mint leaves

prawn won tons with sweet chilli dipping sauce

500 g (1 lb 2 oz) raw prawns (shrimp), peeled, deveined and chopped
2 tablespoons chopped fresh coriander (cilantro)
1 tablespoon oyster sauce
1 teaspoon grated fresh ginger
1 teaspoon sesame oil
½ teaspoon salt
24 won ton wrappers
light-flavoured oil, for frying (I like canola)

sweet chilli dipping sauce
3 large red chillies, finely chopped
250 ml (9 fl oz/1 cup) rice vinegar
2 teaspoons salt
165 g (5¾ oz/¾ cup) sugar
1 large garlic clove, chopped

Mix together the prawns, coriander, oyster sauce, ginger, sesame oil and salt. Put a won ton wrapper on the work surface, place a teaspoonful of filling in the middle, run a wet finger around the edge of the wrapper and then fold it in half to make a triangle. Seal the edges, then fold the top two points of the triangle down over each other to make a shape like a tortellini.

To make the sweet chilli dipping sauce, put all the ingredients in a small saucepan and stir over low heat until the sugar has dissolved. Bring to the boil and cook for 5 minutes or until thickened to a syrupy consistency. Cool before serving.

Heat the oil in a deep-fryer or frying pan over medium heat and deep-fry or shallow-fry the won tons in batches for 2 minutes until golden. Drain on paper towels and serve immediately with the sweet chilli sauce. Makes 24

A very simple but fun way to finish off a Chinese banquet is with thin slices of fresh watermelon and fortune cookies

sticky spare ribs

2 racks pork spare ribs (around 1.3 kg/
  3 lb each)
sea salt
freshly ground black pepper
4 garlic cloves, crushed
2 tablespoons finely grated fresh ginger
250 ml (9 fl oz/1 cup) soy sauce
125 ml (4 fl oz/½ cup) honey
3 tablespoons Shaoxing wine or dry
  sherry
1 teaspoon five-spice
125 ml (4 fl oz/½ cup) hoisin sauce

Preheat the oven to 160°C (315°F/Gas 2–3). Put the ribs on a baking tray and season generously with salt and pepper. Roast for 1 hour.

Meanwhile, put the garlic, ginger, soy sauce, honey, wine, five-spice and hoisin sauce in a small saucepan over medium heat and cook for 15 minutes, stirring occasionally, until thick.

Baste the ribs with the sauce and cook for another 20 minutes. Put the ribs on a chopping board, baste again with the sauce and cut into individual ribs to serve.
Serves 6

rice salad with mint leaves

snow pea salad with sesame seeds

3 baby bok choy (pak choy), halved
300 g (10½ oz) snow peas (mangetout),
  topped and tailed
125 ml (4 fl oz/½ cup) soy sauce
125 ml (4 fl oz/½ cup) mirin
2 teaspoons black sesame seeds

Blanch the bok choy and snow peas in boiling water for 1–2 minutes until just tender
(they should be bright green). Drain and refresh under cold water. Mix together the
bok choy, snow peas, soy sauce, mirin and sesame seeds and refrigerate before
serving. Serves 6

rice salad with mint leaves

750 g (1 lb 10 oz/4 cups) cooked
  short-grain white rice, cooled
3 tablespoons olive oil
2 tablespoons lime juice
sea salt
freshly ground black pepper
3 tablespoons julienned fresh ginger
4 spring onions (scallions), finely sliced
handful fresh mint leaves

Put the rice in a large bowl. Mix together the oil, lime juice, salt and pepper. Add the
ginger, spring onions and mint and toss well with the rice. Serves 6

Don't be scared to have a bit of fun when you're entertaining... choose a theme, pick the music to suit and buy some decorations.

sunday roast roast pork with pear chutney, parsnips with cumin, winter salad with asiago, cabbage with chilli and garlic, bread and butter pudding

The butcher will score and tie the pork for you. You don't need to cook it so much that it starts to dry out: a little hint of pink in the middle is good.

roast pork with pear chutney

800 g (1 lb 12 oz) pears, cored and
  finely sliced
1 white onion, chopped
330 g (11¾ oz/1½ cups) sugar
250 ml (9 fl oz/1 cup) white wine vinegar
¾ teaspoon freshly ground black pepper
3 cinnamon sticks
3 small bay leaves
sea salt

1.8 kg (4 lb) boneless loin of pork,
  scored and tied
1½ tablespoons red wine vinegar

Put the pears, onion, sugar, white wine vinegar, pepper, cinnamon, bay leaves and ¼ teaspoon of salt in a saucepan over medium heat and stir until the sugar has dissolved. Simmer for 40 minutes, or until the chutney is syrupy and the pears are soft and then leave to cool (the chutney will become less runny on cooling).

Preheat the oven to 220°C (425°F/Gas 7). Check the scoring on the pork: for good crackling it should be about 5 mm (¼ inch) deep. Use your fingers to rub the red wine vinegar and salt into the pork skin, making sure the salt gets into the score marks. Put on a rack in a roasting tin and roast for 20 minutes.

Reduce the oven to 200°C (400°F/Gas 6) and roast for another 40–45 minutes, until the juices are almost clear. Let the meat rest out of the oven for 10 minutes before carving and serving with the chutney. Serves 6

parsnips with cumin

1 kg (2 lb 4 oz) parsnips, peeled and
  halved lengthways
2 tablespoons olive oil
1¼ teapoons ground cumin
3 teaspoons fresh thyme

Preheat the oven to 200°C (400°F/Gas 6). Toss the parsnips with the olive oil and cumin and put in a baking tray. Sprinkle with thyme and roast for 45 minutes or until golden. Serve with the roast pork. Serves 6

winter salad with asiago

3 celery stalks, finely sliced
1 baby cos (romaine) lettuce, shredded
½ green apple, finely sliced
sea salt
freshly ground black pepper
2 tablespoons olive oil
1 tablespoon lemon juice
10 thin slices asiago cheese

Put all the ingredients in a large bowl and stir together gently. Serves 6

cabbage with chilli and garlic

2 tablespoons olive oil
1.3 kg (3 lb) cabbage, shredded
1 long red chilli, seeded and thinly sliced
3 garlic cloves, sliced
juice of 2 lemons

Heat a large frying pan, add the oil and heat until very hot. Add the cabbage in batches and cook for 1–2 minutes on each side, or until dark golden, adding a little extra oil if necessary. Transfer the cabbage to a serving bowl.

Add the chilli and garlic to the pan and cook for 1 minute or until golden, then add the lemon juice. Spoon over the cabbage. Serves 6

The winter salad works well as a starter or a side dish to the pork.

bread and butter pudding

125 ml (4 fl oz/½ cup) golden syrup
1 loaf wholemeal (whole-wheat) bread
40 g (1½ oz) butter, softened
40 g (1½ oz/⅓ cup) sultanas (golden
  raisins)
2 eggs, plus 6 egg yolks
500 ml (17 fl oz/2 cups) milk
375 ml (13 fl oz/1½ cups) cream
2 teaspoons natural vanilla extract
115 g (4 oz/½ cup) caster (superfine)
  sugar, plus 1 tablespoon for sprinkling
1 tablespoon orange zest

to serve
cream

Although wholemeal bread isn't traditional, I
love the flavour and richness it adds to this
old nursery pudding.

Lightly grease a 2.5 litre (87 fl oz/10 cup) ovenproof dish and swirl syrup over the
base and side of the dish. Butter the bread, cut each slice in half and arrange one
layer in the bottom of the dish. Sprinkle with some sultanas and top with another layer
of bread. Keep going with the layers until you've used all the bread and sultanas.

Whisk together the eggs, extra yolks, milk, cream, vanilla, sugar and orange zest.
Carefully pour over the bread and leave for 30 minutes. Every 10 minutes or so, press
the bread down so that it soaks up all of the liquid. Sprinkle with the extra sugar.

Preheat the oven to 180ºC (350ºF/Gas 4). Bake the pudding for 50–55 minutes until
golden brown. Leave the pudding out of the oven for 15 minutes to cool a little,
before serving with cream. Serves 6

Make a simple tomato salad by tossing together 3 chopped tomatoes, a small chopped white onion, 1 tablespoon of lime juice and 1 tablespoon of chopped fresh coriander (cilantro) leaves. Season with a pinch of sea salt.

kebab party lamb koftas, bombay potato salad, tuna skewers, fresh mint chutney

lamb koftas

500 g (1 lb 2 oz) minced (ground) lamb
1 teaspoon sea salt
freshly ground black pepper
1 teaspoon ground cumin
1 teaspoon ground coriander
small handful chopped fresh coriander
  (cilantro) leaves
2 white onions, grated
1 small green chilli, finely chopped
2 tablespoons olive oil

to serve
lime wedges
mango chutney

Put the lamb, salt, pepper, cumin, ground coriander, fresh coriander, grated onion and chilli in a bowl and mix together. Shape tablespoons of the mixture into balls and thread onto skewers.

Heat a barbecue or large frying pan over medium–high heat and add the oil. Cook the koftas in batches until browned. Serve with lime wedges and chutney. Serves 4

bombay potato salad

750 g (1 lb 10 oz) waxy potatoes, such
  as kipfler (fingerling), peeled and
  diagonally sliced
1½ teaspoons sea salt
4 tablespoons extra virgin olive oil
3 tablespoons lime juice
2 teaspoons yellow mustard seeds, dry-
  fried for a few seconds until fragrant
2 teaspoons ground turmeric

freshly ground black pepper
1 small green capsicum (pepper), finely
  diced
small handful fresh coriander (cilantro)
  leaves
6 spring onions (scallions), diagonally
  sliced

Bring a large saucepan of water to the boil over high heat. Add the potatoes and 1 teaspoon of salt, reduce the heat to medium and simmer for 8–10 minutes until the potatoes are tender when pierced with a knife. Undercook the potatoes a little because they will continue cooking when removed from the water.

Stir together the olive oil, lime juice, mustard seeds, turmeric, pepper and remaining salt. Pour half the dressing over the hot potatoes and stir gently. Leave to cool, then add the capsicum, coriander, spring onions and remaining dressing and stir gently. Serves 4

tuna skewers

1 tablespoon finely grated fresh ginger
4 garlic cloves, crushed
¼ teaspoon cayenne pepper
1 teaspoon ground coriander
½ teaspoon ground turmeric
1 teaspoon sea salt
freshly ground black pepper
3 tablespoons olive oil
600 g (1 lb 5 oz) tuna, cubed

to serve
lime wedges
fresh coriander (cilantro) sprigs
flat breads
plain yoghurt

Soak eight wooden skewers in water for 1 hour to prevent them scorching. Stir together all the ingredients except the tuna in a bowl. Add the tuna and marinate for 1 hour in the fridge.

Thread the tuna onto the skewers and barbecue or fry over high heat for 1 minute on each side. Serve with lime wedges, coriander, breads and yoghurt. Serves 4

fresh mint chutney

3 large handfuls fresh mint leaves
2 tomatoes, chopped
1 large hot green chilli, chopped
1 clove garlic, chopped
1 tablespoon extra virgin olive oil
1 tablespoon lime juice
sea salt

Wash the mint thoroughly and leave with the water that is clinging to the leaves. Put the tomato in a blender and mix to a purée. Add the mint and remaining ingredients. Blend to a paste, pushing down with a spatula when necessary. Store, covered, in the fridge. Serves 4

Fresh limeade is something a bit different to serve with spicy food. Stir together 4 tablespoons of caster (superfine) sugar and 5 tablespoons of lime juice until the sugar has dissolved. Dilute with mineral water and lots of ice cubes.

Food should always be an adventure and shopping is as much a part of the process as cooking.

To get the seeds from a pomegranate, cut it in half and begin to loosen them up by squeezing firmly. Shake out as many seeds as you can, then cut it open further to separate all the seeds from the pith.

birthday lunch lamb with green olive and walnut relish, potatoes with tomato, feta and parsley, chunky salad, buttermilk puddings with rose-scented raspberries

lamb with green olive and walnut relish

2 lamb backstraps
2 tablespoons olive oil
sea salt
freshly ground black pepper

to serve
green olive and walnut relish, below

Preheat the oven to 240°C (475°F/Gas 8). Brush the lamb with olive oil and sprinkle with salt and pepper. Heat an ovenproof frying pan over high heat until very hot, add the lamb and cook for 2 minutes on one side and 1 minute on the other.

Put the pan of lamb in the oven and cook for 3–5 minutes. Remove from the oven and leave to rest for a few minutes. Cut the lamb into slices on the diagonal and serve with the relish. Serves 4

green olive and walnut relish

175 g (6 oz/1 cup) green olives, pitted
50 g (1¾ oz/½ cup) walnuts
2 tablespoons extra virgin olive oil
2 spring onions (scallions), thinly sliced
3 tablespoons chopped fresh flat-leaf
  (Italian) parsley
1 teaspoon finely chopped green chilli
1 tablespoon pomegranate molasses
1 tablespoon lemon juice
80 g (2¾ oz/½ cup) pomegranate seeds

Roughly chop the olives and walnuts. Stir together with the rest of the ingredients and leave to rest for a while before serving.

potatoes with tomato, feta and parsley

2 tablespoons olive oil
1 red onion, sliced
sea salt
2 garlic cloves, sliced
400 g (14 oz) tin chopped tomatoes, or
    400 ml (14 fl oz) good-quality tomato
    pasta sauce or passata
2 tablespoons fresh flat-leaf (Italian)
    parsley leaves
800 g (1 lb 12 oz) potatoes, peeled and
    cut into wedges

to serve
1 tablespoon lemon juice
100 g (3½ oz) feta cheese, sliced
1 tablespoon fresh flat-leaf (Italian)
    parsley leaves

Heat a large deep frying pan over medium heat. Add the olive oil, onion and a sprinkling of salt and cook for 6–8 minutes until soft. Add the garlic, tomatoes, parsley and 250 ml (9 fl oz/1 cup) of water and bring to the boil. Add the potatoes, cover and cook over low heat for about 20 minutes. Remove the lid, increase the heat a little and cook for another 10 minutes to thicken the sauce. To serve, stir in the lemon juice and top with the feta and extra parsley. Serves 4

chunky salad

2 cucumbers, quartered lengthways and
    then halved
2 baby cos (romaine) lettuces, quartered
small handful fresh mint leaves
3 tablespoons extra virgin olive oil
2 tablespoons lemon juice
sea salt
freshly ground black pepper

Arrange the cucumber, lettuce and mint on a serving platter. Drizzle with the olive oil and lemon juice and sprinkle with sea salt and black pepper. Serves 4

buttermilk puddings with rose-scented raspberries

3 teaspoons powdered gelatine
125 ml (4 fl oz/½ cup) cream
200 g (7 oz) sugar
1 vanilla bean, split lengthways
800 ml (28 fl oz) buttermilk
125 ml (4 fl oz/½ cup) lightly whipped
 cream

to serve
rose-scented raspberries, below

Sprinkle the gelatine over 2 tablespoons of water in a small bowl and set aside. Meanwhile, gently warm the cream, sugar and vanilla bean in a pan until the sugar has dissolved and then remove from the heat. Add the gelatine to the pan, stirring until dissolved. Leave to cool for 10 minutes. Stir in the buttermilk and then fold in the whipped cream.

Pour into six 200 ml (7 fl oz) ramekins and refrigerate for 6 hours or overnight. Top with a spoonful of rose-scented raspberries to serve. Serves 6

rose-scented raspberries

175 g (6 oz/1½ punnets) fresh or frozen
 (and thawed) raspberries
2 tablespoons icing (confectioners')
 sugar, sifted
¾ teaspoon rose water

Put half the raspberries in a glass bowl and crush with a fork. Stir in the icing sugar and taste for sweetness. Fold in the remaining raspberries and the rose water. Chill until you are ready to serve.

moroccan dinner party
pitta bread crisps, roasted red pepper salad, chicken tagine, green beans with watercress, pistachio cake with orange blossom syrup

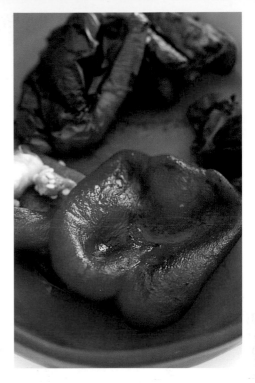

pitta bread crisps

3 rounds wholemeal (whole-wheat) pitta
  bread, split in half and cut into wedges
olive oil, for brushing
sea salt and fennel seeds, for sprinkling

Preheat the oven to 200°C (400°F/Gas 6). Brush the bread with oil and sprinkle with salt and fennel seeds. Bake on a tray for 10 minutes until crisp. Serves 4

You can roast halved capsicums in a hot oven for about 40 minutes or put them under a very hot grill (broiler) for 5 minutes until the skins blacken. Put them in a plastic bag and leave them for 10 minutes and you'll be amazed at how easily the skin peels away.

roasted red pepper salad

3 red capsicums (peppers), roasted, skin
  and seeds removed, cut into strips
3 tomatoes, cored and seeded, cut into
  strips
2 quarters preserved lemon, rinsed,
  pulp removed, finely chopped
2 tablespoons extra virgin olive oil
1 teaspoon lemon juice
freshly ground black pepper

Arrange the capsicum and tomato on a plate, top with the lemon and drizzle with oil and lemon juice. Season with black pepper to serve. Serves 4

I love this meal served outdoors with rugs and cushions strewn around the garden.

When you're making couscous, cover it with boiling water or stock, seal with plastic wrap and don't stir. Once it has absorbed all the liquid, fluff up the grains with a fork.

chicken tagine

8 chicken thighs or legs on the bone,
  skin and fat removed
2 onions, chopped
4 garlic cloves, crushed
1 tablespoon grated fresh ginger
1 teaspoon ground cumin
1 teaspoon paprika
2 pinches saffron threads
115 g (4 oz/½ cup) sliced green olives
1½ tablespoons lemon juice

to serve
couscous

Put the chicken, onions, garlic, ginger, spices and 500 ml (17 fl oz/2 cups) of water in a saucepan and cover with a lid. Bring to the boil then reduce the heat to low. Simmer for 1 hour or until the meat falls off the bone. Stir occasionally, skimming off the excess fat. Increase the heat to high, remove the lid and cook for 15 minutes until the liquid has reduced by half. Stir through the olives and lemon juice. Serve with couscous. Serves 4

green beans with watercress

300 g (10½ oz) baby green beans,
  blanched and refreshed
30 g (1 oz/1 cup) watercress sprigs
3 tablespoons slivered pistachio nuts
2 tablespoons extra virgin olive oil
1 tablespoon lemon juice
sea salt
freshly ground black pepper

Put the beans, watercress, pistachios, oil and juice in a bowl and toss to combine. Season with sea salt and some freshly ground black pepper. Serves 4

pistachio cake with orange blossom syrup

140 g (5 oz/1 cup) pistachio nuts
6 eggs, separated
225 g (8 oz/1 cup) caster (superfine)
  sugar
185 g (6½ oz/¾ cup) plain yoghurt
125 ml (4 fl oz/½ cup) light-flavoured oil
  (I like light olive or canola)
150 g (5½ oz) plain (all-purpose) flour
1 teaspoon baking powder
pinch of salt

to serve
orange blossom syrup, below
figs, halved
plain yoghurt

Preheat the oven to 180°C (350°F/Gas 4). Butter and flour a 26 cm (10½ inch) springform tin and line the base with baking paper. Finely grind the pistachios in a food processor. Beat the egg yolks and half the sugar until pale and very thick. Fold in the yoghurt and oil. Sift the flour, baking powder and salt over the mixture and fold through with the ground pistachios.

Beat the egg whites until soft peaks form. Gradually add the remaining sugar and beat until firm peaks form. Gently fold half into the cake mixture, then fold in the other half. Pour into the tin and bake for 30 minutes. Cover loosely with foil and bake for another 15 minutes, until a skewer poked into the centre comes out clean. Leave to cool completely in the tin and then spoon orange blossom syrup over the top. Serve with fresh figs and yoghurt. Serves 10

orange blossom syrup

225 g (8 oz/1 cup) caster (superfine)
  sugar
125 ml (4 fl oz/½ cup) freshly squeezed
  orange juice
½ teaspoon orange blossom water

Put the sugar, orange juice and 125 ml (4 fl oz/½ cup) of water in a saucepan over low heat and stir to dissolve. Increase the heat and boil for 10–12 minutes, or until syrupy. Remove from the heat and stir in the orange blossom water. Spoon over the cake while the syrup is still warm.

roman holiday roasted olives, marinated parmesan, devil-style chicken, crushed potatoes with garlic and spinach, ricotta fritters with citrus sauce

roasted olives

2 tablespoons olive oil
4 large garlic cloves,
   unpeeled and lightly crushed
2 sprigs fresh rosemary
350 g (12 oz/2 cups) small black olives
4 strips lemon rind

Preheat the oven to 200°C (400°F/Gas 6). Put all the ingredients in a small ovenproof dish and toss together. Roast for 15 minutes and serve warm. Serves 4

marinated parmesan

250 g (9 oz) parmesan cheese
1 garlic clove, crushed
2 tablespoons finely chopped spring
   onions (scallions)
1 teaspoon dried red chilli flakes
125 ml (4 fl oz/½ cup) extra virgin olive
   oil
2 teaspoons finely chopped fresh
   oregano
freshly ground black pepper

to serve
crusty bread

Break the parmesan into small bite-sized pieces. Put in a bowl with the garlic, spring onion, chilli and oil and stir together well. Cover and leave to marinate for at least 2 hours. Just before serving, stir through the oregano and season with black pepper. Serve with warm bread. Serves 4

devil-style chicken

4 x 500 g (1 lb 2 oz) spatchcocks
    (poussin), backbones removed
1 lemon, finely sliced
185 ml (6 fl oz/¾ cup) extra virgin
    olive oil
sea salt
freshly ground black pepper
3 tablespoons lemon juice
2 large red chillies (or to taste),
    seeded and finely chopped

to serve
radicchio leaves

Flatten the spatchcocks with a rolling pin, leaning heavily as you roll. Arrange in a dish and cover with the lemon slices, then add 100 ml (3½ fl oz) of the oil and lots of salt and pepper. Cover and marinate for 30 minutes to an hour.

Heat a large frying pan or barbecue hotplate over medium heat. Put the spatchcocks in the pan (keep the lemon slices from the marinade). Put another frying pan on top of the spatchcocks to squash them and make them really crisp. Cook for 8–10 minutes on each side or until the juices run clear when the thigh is pierced with a fork. Add the lemon slices for the last 5 minutes of cooking, turning them once.

Whisk together the lemon juice, chilli and remaining olive oil to make a dressing. Season with salt and pepper. Chop each spatchcock in half and arrange over the radicchio on a serving platter. Scatter with lemon slices and pour the dressing over the top. Serve with crushed potatoes. Serves 4

crushed potatoes with garlic and spinach

800 g (1 lb 12 oz) new (or
    kipfler/fingerling) potatoes
4 garlic cloves, peeled but left whole
2 teaspoons sea salt

280 g (10 oz) English spinach, shredded
80 ml (2½ fl oz/⅓ cup) cream
2½ tablespoons extra virgin olive oil
freshly ground black pepper

Put the potatoes, garlic and 1 teaspoon of sea salt in a large saucepan and cover with water. Cook for 20 minutes or until the potatoes are just tender when pierced with a skewer. Add the spinach and cook for 1 minute longer. Drain, return to the pan and lightly crush with a potato masher.

Heat the cream and olive oil in a small saucepan over medium heat for 1 minute. Add to the potatoes with the pepper and remaining salt and stir together gently. Serves 4

These fritters were inspired by Marcella Hazan. They are a bit fiddly to make after a meal, so I make the batter before dinner, fry them afterwards and make sure I don't have too much wine during.

ricotta fritters with citrus sauce

250 g (9 oz) fresh ricotta
2 eggs, separated
65 g (2½ oz/½ cup) plain (all-purpose) flour
zest of 1 lemon
pinch of sea salt
40 g (1½ oz/⅓ cup) sultanas (golden raisins)
light-flavoured oil, for frying (I like canola)

to serve
citrus sauce, below

Stir together the ricotta, egg yolks, flour, lemon zest, salt and sultanas. Beat the egg whites until stiff peaks form. Fold through the ricotta mixture.

Heat the oil in a saucepan over medium heat. Drop tablespoons of the mixture into the oil and cook, a few at a time, for 2–3 minutes until golden brown. Remove from the pan with a slotted spoon and drain on paper towels while you cook the rest. Serve immediately, drizzled with citrus sauce. Serves 4

citrus sauce

225 g (8 oz/1 cup) caster (superfine) sugar
125 ml (4 fl oz/½ cup) lemon juice
1½ tablespoons lemon zest

Put the sugar and 125 ml (4 fl oz/½ cup) of water in a small deep saucepan over hight heat and boil without stirring. Brush the side of the pan with a wet pastry brush to prevent the sugar crystalizing. Once the caramel turns a rich golden colour, remove from the heat and add the lemon juice and zest. The caramel will splatter, so stand back. Stir gently until the sauce is smooth. Serves 4

I don't tend to eat a lot of fried foods, but these are so delicious I make an exception.

retro dinner party prawn, avocado and grapefruit cocktail, roast beef wrapped in prosciutto, potato gratin, strawberries with chantilly cream, chocolate truffles

prawn, avocado and grapefruit cocktail

1 butter lettuce
1 large ripe avocado, sliced
1 pink grapefruit, segmented, pith
  removed, reserving 1 tablespoon
  of juice for the dressing
16 cooked prawns (shrimp), peeled and
  deveined but tails left intact

to serve
cocktail dressing, below

Arrange the lettuce in four dishes. Top with the avocado, grapefruit and prawns and drizzle with the dressing to serve. Serves 4

To slice an avocado cleanly and neatly, cut it in half and remove the seed. Slice it into thin wedges (squeeze a lemon over the top to stop it turning brown) and then use a sharp knife to slice the flesh away from the peel.

cocktail dressing

1 egg yolk
1 tablespoon dijon mustard
1 pinch cayenne pepper or dash
  of Tabasco sauce
3 tablespoons light-flavoured oil (I like
  grapeseed or vegetable)
2 tablespoons tomato sauce (ketchup)
2 teaspoons worcestershire sauce
1 teaspoon Cognac or brandy
1 tablespoon grapefruit juice
sea salt
freshly ground black pepper

Whisk the egg yolk, mustard and pepper in a bowl. Add the oil in a slow, steady stream, whisking constantly until all of the oil is combined and the dressing thickens. Stir in the tomato sauce, worcestershire sauce, Cognac and grapefruit juice and season with salt and pepper.

Liven up fresh peas by serving them with white onion and mint leaves. Soften the chopped onion in olive oil for 5 minutes, add 4 tablespoons chicken stock and bring to the boil. Add 2½ cups of fresh or frozen peas and cook, covered, for 3–5 minutes. Serve with a knob of butter and shredded mint leaves.

roast beef wrapped in prosciutto

1 kg (2 lb 4 oz) beef fillet
sea salt
freshly ground black pepper
2 tablespoons olive oil
9–12 long slices prosciutto
1 tablespoon dijon mustard

to serve
dijon mustard
peas with onion and mint, left

Preheat the oven to 180°C (350°F/Gas 4). Season the beef fillet with salt and pepper and rub with the olive oil. Heat a large frying pan over high heat. When very hot, sear the beef on all sides until browned and then allow to cool a little. Arrange the prosciutto slices, overlapping slightly to make a large rectangle, on a piece of non-stick paper and spread with mustard. Put the beef on top and bring the prosciutto up over the sides of the beef to enclose it. Tie with kitchen string.

Roast the beef for 25 minutes (for medium–rare meat). Remove from the oven, cover with foil and leave to rest in a warm place for 5–10 minutes. Slice the meat, drizzle with the pan juices and serve with mustard and peas. Serves 4

potato gratin

1 garlic clove, peeled and cut in half
butter, for greasing
1 kg (2 lb 4 oz) all-purpose potatoes
 (I like desiree or pontiac)
375 ml (13 fl oz/1½ cups) milk
125 ml (4 fl oz/½ cup) cream or crème
 fraîche
100 g (3½ oz) gruyère cheese, grated
sea salt
freshly ground black pepper

Preheat the oven to 180°C (350°F/Gas 4). Rub the inside of a 1.5 litre (52 fl oz/6 cup) ovenproof dish with garlic and then grease with butter. Peel and very thinly slice the potatoes (use a mandolin if you have one). Put the potatoes in a bowl with the milk, cream and half the cheese. Season and toss together well. Transfer to the dish, top with the remaining cheese and bake for 1 hour 15 minutes. Serves 4

strawberries with chantilly cream

250 ml (9 fl oz/1 cup) cream
2 tablespoons caster (superfine) sugar
1 teaspoon natural vanilla extract
500 g (1 lb 2 oz/2 punnets) perfect
  strawberries, hulled and halved if large

to serve
icing (confectioners') sugar, for dusting

Whisk together the cream, caster sugar and vanilla until soft peaks form.
Do not over-whisk.

Pile the strawberries into serving dishes, sift a little icing sugar over them and top with
chantilly cream. Serves 4

chocolate truffles

200 g (7 oz) good-quality dark
  chocolate, finely chopped
125 ml (4 fl oz/½ cup) cream
icing (confectioners') sugar, for dusting
cocoa powder, sifted, for coating

Line a baking tray with baking paper or plastic wrap. Put the chocolate in a large
heatproof bowl. Heat the cream to scalding point in a small saucepan, then quickly
pour it over the chocolate. Mix thoroughly until all the chocolate has melted and the
mixture is smooth. Set aside to cool, then refrigerate for about 30 minutes.

When the mixture is set, dust your hands with some icing sugar to prevent the
chocolate sticking, then roll the mixture into small balls. Immediately roll the truffles
in cocoa powder and place them on the baking tray. Refrigerate to set for a further
30 minutes. Makes 18

I finish off my truffles with the best-quality
cocoa powder I can find. I really notice
the difference.

Don't be scared of the classics — they're old favourites
for a reason.

anchovy and red onion toasts

catalan dinner anchovy and red onion toasts, blood orange and fennel salad, butterflied lamb with romesco sauce, virgin paella, crema catalana

anchovy and red onion toasts

small sourdough bagette, cut into
  18 slices
olive oil, for brushing
small handful fresh flat-leaf (Italian)
  parsley, chopped
2½ tablespoons chopped red onion
1 tablespoon lemon zest
18 anchovy fillets

Preheat the oven to 200°C (400°F/Gas 6). Put the sourdough slices on a baking tray and brush lightly with olive oil on both sides. Cook for 5–7 minutes, or until crisp and lightly golden. Mix together the parsley, onion, lemon zest and anchovies and spoon on top of the toasts. Makes 18

blood orange and fennel salad

6 blood oranges, peeled and sliced
2 baby fennel, finely sliced
85 g (3 oz/½ cup) small black olives
4 radishes, finely sliced
large handful wild rocket (arugula)

3 tablespoons extra virgin olive oil
2 tablespoons red wine vinegar
sea salt
freshly ground black pepper

Arrange the orange and fennel slices on serving plates. Top with the olives, radishes and rocket. Drizzle the olive oil and vinegar over the salad and season with salt and pepper. Serves 6

butterflied lamb with romesco sauce

1.8 kg (4 lb) butterflied lamb leg, cut into
  two pieces
3 tablespoons olive oil
sea salt
freshly ground black pepper

to serve
romesco sauce, below
lemon wedges
small handful fresh flat-leaf (Italian)
  parsley

virgin paella

Preheat the oven to 180ºC (350ºF/Gas 4). Heat an ovenproof frying pan over high heat. Rub the lamb with the oil and season well. Put the lamb skin side down in the pan and sear for 5 minutes, then turn over and cook for 2 minutes. Put the pan in the oven and roast for 15 minutes. Cover loosely with foil and rest for 10 minutes. Slice thickly and serve with romesco sauce, lemon wedges and parsley. Serves 6

romesco sauce

4 red capsicums (peppers), peeled and
  seeded
4 tablespoons blanched almonds,
  toasted

1 tablespoon red wine vinegar
2 tablespoons extra virgin olive oil
sea salt
freshly ground black pepper

Put all the ingredients in a blender and pulse until the sauce is combined but still has some texture.

virgin paella

1 tablespoon olive oil
1 white onion, chopped
425 g (15 oz/2 cups) paella rice
125 ml (4½ fl oz/½ cup) white wine
1.25 litres (44 fl oz/5 cups) chicken
  stock

6 saffron threads
sea salt

Heat the oil in a large, heavy-based deep frying pan or paella pan over low-medium heat and cook the onion for 5 minutes until soft and golden. Add the rice and cook for 1 minute, stirring to coat. Add the wine and cook for 1 minute. Add the stock and saffron and cook, stirring occasionally, for 15 minutes or until the rice is just cooked. Season with salt and serve. Serves 6

Chilled rosé works wonderfully with this meal.

crema catalana

625 ml (21½ fl oz/2½ cups) cream
170 ml (5½ fl oz/⅔ cup) milk
2 teaspoons natural vanilla extract
2 cinnamon sticks
peel from 1 orange
peel from 1 lemon
6 egg yolks
4 tablespoons caster (superfine) sugar
2½ tablespoons soft brown sugar

Preheat the oven to 140°C (275°F/Gas 1). Put the cream, milk, vanilla extract, cinnamon, orange and lemon peel in a saucepan over medium heat and bring just to boiling point, then remove from the heat.

Whisk together the egg yolks and caster sugar in a large bowl. Strain the cream and pour slowly over the yolk and sugar mixture, whisking constantly. Skim off any foam that rises to the top.

Put six 125 ml (4 fl oz/½ cup) ramekins in a large roasting tin and spoon the mixture into the ramekins. Pour hot water into the tin to come halfway up the sides of the ramekins and cover the whole tin with foil. Bake for 30–35 minutes, or until just set. Lift the ramekins out of the roasting tin and leave to cool before chilling in the fridge for 2 hours.

Preheat the grill (broiler) to its hottest temperature. Put the ramekins on a baking tray, sprinkle brown sugar over the chilled creams and then place under the grill for a couple of minutes until the sugar is melted and dark golden (if you have a chef's blowtorch, this is the time to use it). Leave for a few minutes for the sugar to cool and harden before serving. Serves 6

I start with a shopping list but usually buy
hardly anything on it. I'm just inspired by what
I see and the journey starts there.

lunch with a greek theme braised chicken with lemon and honey, shepherd's salad with feta, vanilla rice pudding, baked rhubarb

braised chicken with lemon and honey

1 tablespoon olive oil
1 x 1.6 kg (3 lb 8 oz) chicken, cut into
 8 pieces
1 red onion, sliced
12 garlic cloves, peeled but left whole
1 lemon, cut into chunks
185 ml (6 fl oz/¾ cup) chicken stock
125 g (4½ oz/½ cup) honey
small handful fresh oregano leaves

Heat a large frying pan over high heat, add the oil and chicken and cook for 5 minutes until golden. Remove and set aside. Reduce the heat to medium–high, add the onion and cook for 1 minute. Add the garlic and cook for 1 minute.

Return the chicken to the pan with the lemon, chicken stock and honey, reduce the heat, cover the pan and simmer for 20 minutes or until the chicken is cooked through. Lift out the chicken and put on a baking tray. Increase the heat under the sauce, and simmer, uncovered, for another 15 minutes to thicken. Place the chicken under a hot grill (broiler) until crisp. Arrange the chicken on a platter, drizzle with the sauce and sprinkle with oregano. Serves 4

shepherd's salad with feta

400 g (14 oz) tin chickpeas, rinsed and
 drained
150 g (5½ oz) feta cheese, crumbled
small handful fresh flat-leaf (Italian)
 parsley
2 Lebanese cucumbers, chopped
1 green capsicum (pepper), chopped
50 g (1¾ oz/⅓ cup) black olives, halved
 and pitted

dressing
3 tablespoons olive oil
1 tablespoon lemon juice
sea salt
freshly ground black pepper

Gently mix together the chickpeas, feta, parsley, cucumber, capsicum and olives in a large bowl. To make the dressing, whisk the olive oil and lemon juice and season with salt and pepper. Toss the dressing with the salad. Serves 4

vanilla rice pudding

1 litre (35 fl oz/4 cups) milk
75 g (2¾ oz/⅓ cup) sugar
2 strips orange rind
1 vanilla bean, scraped (or 1 teaspoon
  natural vanilla extract)
180 g (6½ oz) arborio rice
3 egg yolks

to serve
baked rhubarb, below
cream, optional

Put the milk, sugar, orange rind, vanilla bean and seeds in a saucepan and bring to a simmer over medium heat. Add the rice and stir occasionally to prevent it catching on the bottom of the pan. Cook for 30 minutes, or until the rice is tender. Add the egg yolks one at a time, mixing well. Remove from the heat and leave to stand for 5 minutes. Remove the orange zest and vanilla bean. Spoon into serving bowls and top with baked rhubarb and cream. Serves 4

baked rhubarb

500 g (1 lb 2 oz/1 bunch) rhubarb
115 g (4 oz/½ cup) caster (superfine)
  sugar

Preheat the oven to 180°C (350°F/Gas 4). Trim away the base and leaves from the rhubarb and rinse the stems. Cut the rhubarb stems into short lengths and toss thoroughly with the sugar. Transfer the rhubarb to a stainless steel, non-stick or ceramic baking dish, making sure it is covered with sugar. Cover tightly with foil and bake for 35–45 minutes or until soft.

Let the rhubarb cool in the syrup that has formed. Spoon the syrup over the rhubarb as it is cooling (this will give it a bright even colour). Serves 4

bistro lunch herbed chicken schnitzel, fennel 'slaw, apple and pistachio galette

herbed chicken schnitzel

4 chicken breasts, skin removed
60 g (2¼ oz/½ cup) plain (all-purpose) flour
freshly ground black pepper
sea salt
1 egg
2 tablespoons milk
160 g (5¾ oz/2 cups) fresh breadcrumbs

3 tablespoons chopped fresh flat-leaf (Italian) parsley
3 tablespoons chopped fresh chervil
3 tablespoons chopped fresh oregano
1 tablespoon butter
125 ml (4 fl oz/½ cup) olive oil

to serve
mashed potatoes, right

Put each chicken breast between two sheets of plastic wrap and flatten slightly with a meat mallet or rolling pin. Cut each flattened breast in half. Put the flour in a shallow bowl and season with pepper and 1 teaspoon of salt. In a second bowl, lightly beat the egg and milk together. Mix the breadcrumbs and herbs in a third bowl and season with salt and pepper. Dip each chicken fillet in flour to coat, then in the egg mixture and lastly in the breadcrumbs.

Heat the butter and olive oil in a large non-stick frying pan over medium heat and cook the schnitzels for 3 minutes on each side until golden brown and cooked through (don't overcrowd the pan: cook them in batches if necessary). Drain on paper towels and keep warm until all the chicken is cooked. Serves 4

Schnitzels are great with mash. Peel and chop 800 g (1 lb 12 oz) of mashing potatoes (such as pontiac) and boil until tender. Drain, return to the hot pan and mash. Heat 185 ml (6 fl oz/¾ cup) milk or cream, 80 g (2¾ oz) of butter and a pinch of sea salt in a pan until hot. Beat into the potatoes with a wooden spoon until smooth.

fennel 'slaw

3 fennel bulbs, finely sliced
2 tablespoons small salted capers, rinsed
1 small red onion, finely sliced
1½ tablespoons chopped fresh flat-leaf (Italian) parsley
3 tablespoons whole-egg mayonnaise
1½ tablespoons lemon juice
sea salt
freshly ground black pepper

Put the fennel, capers, onion and parsley in a bowl. Mix together the mayonnaise and lemon juice and stir through the 'slaw. Season with sea salt and black pepper to serve. Serves 4

I like to use ligurian honey from Kangaroo Island off South Australia. If you can't buy that, try lavender or blue gum honey or just your favourite runny variety.

apple and pistachio galette

375 g (13 oz) puff pastry
1 egg yolk, beaten
frangipane, below
2 green apples, peeled, quartered, cored
  and thinly sliced
melted butter, for brushing
1 tablespoon ligurian honey

to serve
ligurian honey
chopped pistachio nuts, shelled and
  unsalted
vanilla ice cream

Preheat the oven to 220°C (425°F/Gas 7). Roll out the pastry to 3 mm (⅛ inch) thick and then trim to 22 x 30 cm (8½ x 12 inches) to help the pastry rise evenly. Place on a paper-lined baking tray. Use the point of a sharp knife to score a 1 cm (½ inch) border around the edge of the pastry, being careful not to cut all the way through. Prick the centre all over with a fork and brush with egg yolk.

Spread the frangipane evenly over the pastry within the scored area. Layer the apple slices over the top, brush lightly with melted butter and bake for 15 minutes. Reduce the oven to 200°C (400°F/Gas 6). Drizzle with the honey and bake for another 15 minutes or until golden. Drizzle with the extra honey, sprinkle with pistachios and serve immediately with a scoop of vanilla ice cream. Serves 6

frangipane

3 tablespoons pistachio nuts, shelled
  and unsalted
3 tablespoons ground almonds
40 g (1½ oz) unsalted butter, softened
3 tablespoons caster (superfine) sugar
1 egg yolk
¼ teaspoon natural vanilla extract

Crush the pistachio nuts with a rolling pin and then fold together thoroughly with the remaining ingredients.

bill's library

I thank all of these talented authors for their constant inspiration.

Amad, Abla, *The Lebanese Kitchen*, Viking, Melbourne, 2001

Alexander, Stephanie, *The Cook's Companion*, Viking, Melbourne, 1996

Beranbaum, Rose Levy, *The Pie And Pastry Bible*, Scribner, New York, 1998

Beranbaum, Rose Levy, *The Cake Bible, William Morrow*, New York, 1998

David, Elizabeth, *Elizabeth David Classics*, Grub Street, London, 1999

Dupleix, Jill, *Old Food*, Allen & Unwin, 1998

Hazan, Marcella, *The Classic Italian Cookbook*, Papermac, London, 1980

Hazan, Marcella, *The Essentials of Classic Italian Cooking*, Macmillan, London, 1992

Jaffrey, Madhur, *Ultimate Curry Bible*, Random House, London 2003

Roden, Claudia, *The Food of Italy*, Vintage, London, 1999

Roden, Claudia, *Mediterranean Cookery*, BBC Books, London, 1987

Solomon, Charmaine, *Encyclopedia of Asian Food*, William Heinemann Australia, Melbourne, 1996

Time-Life Series, *The Good Cook Series*, Chief Consultant Richard Olney, Time-Life Books, Amsterdam, 1978–1982

Waters, Alice, *Chez Panisse Café Cookbook*, HarperCollins, New York, 1999

Waters, Alice, *Chez Panisse Desserts*, Random House, New York, 1985

Wells, Patricia, *At Home in Provence*, Kyle Cathie, London, 1998

Wells, Patricia, *The Provence Cookbook*, HarperCollins, New York 2004

Wells, Patricia, *Trattoria*, Kyle Cathie, London, 1993

Wolfert, Paula, *The Cooking of the Eastern Mediterranean*, HarperCollins, New York, 1994

Wolfert, Paula, *Mediterranean Cooking*, HarperCollins, New York, 1994

Wolfert, Paula, *Mostly Mediterranean,* Penguin Books, New York, 1998

index

FOR NATALIE, EDIE, INES AND BUNNY

Published by Murdoch Books Pty Limited.

Murdoch Books Pty Limited Australia
Pier 8/9, 23 Hickson Road, Millers Point NSW 2000
Phone: +61 (0)2 8220 2000 Fax: +61 (0)2 8220 2558

Murdoch Books UK Limited
Erico House, 6th Floor North, 93–99 Upper Richmond Road
Putney, London SW15 2TG
Phone: +44 (0)20 8785 5995 Fax: +44 (0)20 8785 5985

Chief Executive: Juliet Rogers
Publisher: Kay Scarlett

Editor: Jane Price
Photographer: Petrina Tinslay
Styling and Photographic Art Direction: Marcus Hay
Design Concept: Eskimo Design
Designer: Annette Fitzgerald
Food Editor and Food Styling: Sonia Greig
Food Preparation: Lee Husband
Production: Monika Paratore
Styling Assistance: Tamara Boon, Tanya Laycock

The publisher and stylist would like to thank the following for their generosity in supplying furniture, props and kitchenware for this book: Alex Liddy; Arte Flowers; Bison; David Edmonds; Design Mode International; Deborah Hutton Living; Dinosaur Designs, Essential Ingredient; G&C Ventura, HWI; IKEA; Jurass, Koziol, Lotus, Mitchell & Helen English; Mud Australia; Orrefors Kosta Boda; Orson & Blake; Papaya; Plenty; Simon Johnson; Spence & Lyda; The Sydney Antique Centre; Villeroy & Boch; Waterford Wedgwood; Wheel & Barrow; fabric supplied by Chee Soon & Fitzgerald, Cloth and Signature Prints; candles supplied by Stax of Wax; paint supplied by Porter's Paints; clothes supplied by Flying Standard, Marcs, Orson & Blake Basement and Worling Saunders; furniture supplied by ECC Lighting & Living, Ici et la, Norman & Quaine, Space, Spence and Lyda, Stylecraft, and Orson & Blake; flowers supplied by Grandiflora; surfboard supplied by Justin Lee; hair and make-up by Greg Ruggeri.

National Library of Australia Cataloguing-in-Publication Data
Granger, Bill, 1969- . Simply Bill. Includes index.
ISBN 1 74045 363 8. 1. Cookery. I. Title. 641.5

Printed by 1010 Printing Limited in 2005. PRINTED IN HONG KONG.
First published 2005.
Text copyright © Bill Granger
Design and photography copyright © Murdoch Books Pty Limited 2005

IMPORTANT: Those who might be at risk from the effects of salmonella poisoning (the elderly, pregnant women, young children and those suffering from immune deficiency diseases) should consult their doctor with any concerns about eating raw eggs.

CONVERSION GUIDE: You may find cooking times vary depending on the oven you are using. For fan-forced ovens, as a general rule, set the oven temperature to 20°C (35°F) lower than indicated in the recipe. We have used 20 ml (4 teaspoon) tablespoon measures. If you are using a 15 ml (3 teaspoon) tablespoon, for most recipes the difference will not be noticeable. However, for recipes using baking powder, gelatine, bicarbonate of soda (baking soda) or small amounts of cornflour (cornstarch), add an extra teaspoon for each tablespoon specified. We have used 59 g (2 oz) eggs.